FINDING
FAVOUR *with the*
KING

PREPARING FOR YOUR MOMENT
IN HIS PRESENCE

TOMMY
TENNEY

Books by Tommy Tenney

TOMMY TENNEY

FINDING FAVOUR *with the*
KING

PREPARING FOR YOUR MOMENT IN HIS PRESENCE

BETHANYHOUSE

MINNEAPOLIS, MINNESOTA

Published by Bethany House Publishers
11400 Hampshire Avenue South
Bloomington, Minnesota 55438
www.bethanyhouse.com

Bethany House Publishers is a Division of
Baker Book House Company, Grand Rapids, Michigan.

Printed in the United States of America

ISBN 0-7642-2735-1 (Hard cover)
ISBN 0-7642-2860-9 (Audiobook)
ISBN 0-7642-2871-4 (International Trade Paper)

Library of Congress Cataloging-in-Publication Data

Tenney, Tommy, 1956-
    Finding favor with the King : preparing for your moment in his presence / by Tommy Tenney
     p.   cm.
Includes bibliographical references.
    ISBN 0-7642-2735-1 (alk. paper)
    1. Bible. O.T. Esther—Criticism, interpretation, etc.   I. Title.
    BS1375.52T46   2003
    222'.906—dc21

                                                 2003013799

CONTENTS

CONNECT
WITH
TOMMY
TENNEY

Have you ever read a book and wished that you could remember all the things you learned from its pages? Reading a book and applying the knowledge gained from that book are two different things.

I want to help you "find favor" by applying the principles found in this book!

To assist you in continuing your journey into the King's palace, I have created a special interactive online Esther experience! It's like a roadmap of sorts. There is a ...

- special study guide
- audio streaming, and
- printable "Protocols of the Palace" artwork.

Also available is an Esther devotional sent to you daily by e-mail. I want you to succeed!

If you can't access the GodChasers.network Web site, we can ship you a free teaching CD or tape, "Lessons From Esther," for a minimal shipping charge.

Visit **www.godchasers.net** and download your FREE audio lesson & Study Guide! Available online only!

GodChasers.network
The ministry of Tommy Tenney
PO Box 3355
Pineville, LA 71361
1-888-433-3355 or 1-318-442-4273
www.godchasers.net

To the ones who taught me most.
The *four queens* of my life.
I can't imagine life in my humble "palace" without them.
My three daughters and my wife.
May I rise to the level of their royalty.

CHAPTER 1

FROM PEASANT TO PRINCESS

What a Difference a Day Makes!

INTRODUCTION

D ivine secrets of transformation await you in this life-and-death saga from Esther's pre-Islamic Persia. It is here that God uses the most unlikely of heroes to save His people from genocide at the hands of a powerful and highly placed madman named Haman. Not only did God use unlikely heroes—but He also used unlikely weapons!

How does this story from the antiquity of ancient Iraq apply to us *today*? If it was a mere children's story, it wouldn't apply at all. But it isn't. This story has the feel of a fairy tale!

Hidden among the secrets of palace protocol is an encoded portrayal of Bible purpose—*access to God's presence*. The book of Esther literally contains a spiritual roadmap to God! We cannot afford to shrug off this story as something we heard about in church decades ago or dismiss it as some "irrelevant Old Testament book."

God reveals through Esther's life just how He worked through one young woman to save the Jewish people from total annihilation by an impossibly powerful leader. Esther's story reveals eternal wisdom about *your own future and destiny*!

Most little girls I've known have dreamed of becoming a princess (most young boys secretly dream of being a king too). The "princess and king" dream lives on into adulthood for most of us. Why else would the contemporary world be so captivated by the storybook wedding of Princess Diana to Prince Charles years ago?

An estimated 750 million people in seventy-four countries dropped what they were doing and crowded around television sets to watch the ceremony of the first English woman to marry an heir to the British throne in over three hundred years. Every eye followed Lady Diana as she walked down the aisle of St. Paul's Cathedral in a royal procession to meet Prince Charles. In the words of the archbishop of Canterbury, "Here is the stuff of which fairy tales are made."[1]

Otherwise happy and contented women around the globe suddenly felt the familiar pangs of their childhood, longing to be a "princess bride" once again. Very few modern nations or cultures continue to have royalty or princesses, but little girls *still* dream of one day being a princess bride, and little boys *still* imagine becoming a king.

Is it any accident that the dream of a "princess bride" is so persistent even in contemporary societies, generations after true earthly royalty became rare?

Could it be that our Creator planted this dream deep inside our hearts as a hidden seed, an eternal dream waiting to be fulfilled at just the right time? This dream has divine destiny at its core.

Authors, playwrights, and poets in virtually every culture since the beginning of human history have dabbled with the theme of commoners morphing into royalty at the whim of a king. Hans Christian Andersen penned his renowned children's story "The Ugly Duckling," describing the miraculous transformation of an "ugly duckling" into what it was always intended to be, a beautiful swan.

How many of us can still recite the theme and story line of Cinderella's transformation from lowly youngest sister to queen of the land?

Proof of the multigenerational intrigue of the fairy-tale stories is founded on the fact that accounts like this continue to be bestsellers. It is amazing that such an ancient theme would have such enduring interest—whether in the form of Cinderella, King Arthur, or the contemporary Broadway production of *The King and I*.

The sensational elevation of a common person into royalty ignites the dreams of potential in every one of us.

OUR FASCINATION WITH ELEVATION IS A GOD THING

Perhaps the most intriguing of these fairy-tale transformations is found in the biblical account of Esther. In fact, the story of Esther is far more ancient and powerful than any of the more recent transformation tales.

It is the true story of a young Jewish peasant girl who is herded through the back door of a Persian king's palace and wins his heart to become queen against all odds and save her nation. The biblical account of Esther has convinced me that our lifelong fascination with transformation through love and choice is a "God thing."

If the story of Esther portrays a peasant who became a princess, then the story of her predecessor portrays the fall of a regal Persian queen to a lowly commoner (and possibly a dead one at that)!

Long before Esther was suddenly elevated to princess and then queen of Persia, another queen, named Vashti, fell from grace.

> On the seventh day, when the heart of the king [Xerxes] was merry with wine, he commanded . . . seven eunuchs who served in [his] presence . . . to bring Queen Vashti before the king, wearing her royal crown, in order to show her beauty to the people and the officials, for she was beautiful to behold. *But Queen Vashti refused to come at the king's command* brought by his eunuchs; therefore *the king was furious,* and his anger burned within him.[2]

VASHTI'S PLACE WAS GIVEN TO ANOTHER

No one really knows why Queen Vashti refused to obey the command of King Xerxes. Nor do we know what actually happened to her. The account in the book of Esther simply says that she would come before the king no more and that her place would be given to someone who was better than she.[3]

Many believe Queen Vashti was demoted and banished or allowed to stay out of sight in the women's area of the palace. Some believe she was quickly executed in the same way that so many others were summarily "removed from Xerxes' sight" for offending the self-proclaimed "Lord of Lords."

Perhaps a hood was placed over Vashti's face, in the same way the king's bodyguards later handled Haman. (The Bible says the fate of Haman, the enemy of Mordecai and the Jews, was sealed suddenly: "As soon as the king spoke, his attendants *covered Haman's face, signaling his doom.*"[4])

It is not uncommon—even in modern executions—for a hood to be placed over the face of the accused. In ancient Persia, this occurred immediately upon sentencing. It meant your fate was sealed—you would never again see the king's face.

This same king, on a later day, would hold the fate of Esther and of all her people suspended in his hand with a golden scepter. We see several times in the Esther story that King Xerxes ordered the execution of enemies and seditious plotters without a second thought.

Considering the pattern of the king of Persia, it is even more amazing that Queen Vashti challenged his authority. In fact, she did far more than simply say no to her husband's request. She publicly scorned his authority in front of the top army commanders, political officials, and leading citizens of Persia.

Even worse, she did it in front of everyone at the grand climax of his 180-day banquet and council to drum up support for war against the Greeks. (Personally, I'm fairly confident that King Xerxes' seven top advisors quickly and chauvinistically eliminated Queen Vashti to make an example of her before the king could come to his senses.)

This is the danger-fraught stage onto which the peasant girl Esther would enter. Her introduction to the palace would place her in an environment where the slightest word could lead to the greatest humiliation—*or elevation!* Esther's story is *more* than a tale of palace intrigue, abduction, murder, assassination plots, genocide, and impossible romance on the edge of life and death.

THE POTENTIAL OF PROMOTION

Again, God reveals through Esther's life just how He worked through one young woman to save the Jewish people from total annihilation by an incredibly powerful leader. Esther's story reveals eternal wisdom about *our own future and destiny!*

How will people of destiny be transformed from their "peasant" state into a royal bride without spot or wrinkle? Perhaps the answer may be found in pursuing a second question: How could a mere peasant's passion for the king transform her into a princess?

The answers to *both questions* are hidden in the book of Esther. If we are to be the bride of the King, perhaps we should take some notes from Esther's rags-to-riches, pauper-to-princess miracle.[5]

Most of us want to *be* more and *live* better than we do at the moment. Many of us live with the knowledge that we claim royal rank, but we act like someone more at home in the common surroundings of the world. People often have a hard time seeing any differences between us and those who make no claim to know God.

The genius of the book of Esther is its revelation of *the way God overcomes human weakness and failure to elevate our position and rank all the way to His throne room.* Esther gazed into the king's eyes, captured his heart, and found his favor. Then she was transported from the hall of women to the house of the king as his queen.

EVIL HAS ALWAYS FEARED
ESTHER'S STORY[6]

Even Hitler and the Nazi concentration camp commanders feared the power of the book of Esther. In fact, they banned it in their death camps! One writer noted:

Anti-Semites have always hated the book, and the Nazis forbade its reading in the crematoria and the concentration camps. In the dark days before their deaths, Jewish inmates of Auschwitz, Dachau, Treblinka, and Bergen-Belsen wrote the Book of Esther from memory and read it in secret on Purim. Both they and their brutal foes understood its message. This unforgettable book teaches that Jewish resistance to annihilation, then as now, represents the service of God and devotion to His cause. In every age, *martyrs and heroes, as well as ordinary men and women, have seen in it not merely a record of past deliverance but a prophecy of future salvation.*[7]

Evil *still* fears Esther's story today—it *reveals divinity's solution for humanity's confusion.* This short story holds secrets to salvage broken lives, shattered destinies, and fallen dreams.

You may feel trapped in the kingdom of the workplace under a tyrannical "king" of your own. Who knows but that you came to such a place "for such a time as this"? The revelation of Esther can preserve you, yes, but it can also "present" you and change your future.

Satan has his own concentration camps—he is a practitioner of his own form of ethnic cleansing. He wants to exterminate from the globe every child of the King, along with their children. And he would still ban the message of Esther from as many as possible. Esther's story is a prophecy of future doom to Satan's plans. It is also a prophecy of divine transformation and elevation to all who learn its lessons.

WAS IT ESTHER'S BEAUTY, HER SECRET, OR BOTH?

So why was a peasant girl from a nation in exile chosen as queen by a powerful Persian king? Why did Xerxes pass over as many as *1,459 other candidates* from other nations and Persia's own 127 province-nations to select Esther?[8] Was it just because of her beauty, *or did she know a secret*?

Could it be that God orchestrated Esther's life to reveal what can happen at a divine intersection *where potential meets protocol*? Who knows what can happen in your life when preparation intersects with protocol and destiny is birthed?

According to rabbinic tradition, Esther was one of the four most beautiful Jewish women of all time (the others were Sarah, Rahab, and Abigail).[9] King Xerxes had unlimited access to the most beautiful women in the world, and his extensive harem system was proof of it.

It would take more than outward beauty or sensual appeal to captivate such a man. Xerxes could have had Esther remain a concubine or secondary wife, yet there was something about her that enticed commitment from him.

Persian kings generally selected their queens from *Persian* royal families, and hopefully from the families of the king's top seven advisors.[10] They could have as many secondary wives or concubines as they wanted, with no restrictions on their nationality or religion, because the offspring from these secondary wives had no right to ascend to the throne.

Esther was an outsider, born not of nobility but of an exiled people! She had none of these things going for her, but somehow she won the heart and then the ear of the king in spite of Persian prejudices and traditions.[11] Have you ever felt like an outsider? What was Esther's secret? If she was chosen, so can you be chosen!

SHOUTED DEMANDS AND FORMAL REQUESTS

Never underestimate the potential of one encounter. Never underestimate the potential of one service or one worship encounter. A few moments in the presence of the King can change your destiny. It only took *one night with the king* to turn a peasant into a princess! One night with a king changes everything!

Remember, though, that Esther spent a full year in intense preparation for that one night with destiny. One year preparing for one night![12] (Have you ever noticed how long it takes a young girl to prepare for a "night out"? Often the importance of the "night" can be measured by the length of preparation.)

I am amazed every time I see a news report or magazine article describing the preparations made by cities, towns, and governments when the president of the United States announces he is coming. It doesn't matter whether it's Boston, Tulsa, or Berlin: *Preparation mirrors the importance of the visit!*

The Bible is full of spectacular romances. We learn about preparation through the sometimes painful but God-ordained romances of the patriarchs: Abraham, Isaac, and Jacob.

We learn even more through the marriages of Salmon and Rahab (who was formerly the Canaanite harlot of Jericho) and of Boaz and Ruth (who was the Moabite widow, and daughter-in-law of Naomi). Both of these marriages between Jewish men and non-Jewish women seemed to go squarely against the accepted norm. Nevertheless they were God-directed unions, because both couples produced children who were in the direct lineage, the family tree, of Jesus Christ.[13]

David and his son Solomon had spectacular loves and dismal marital failures. Their lives are often highlighted and used as extravagant examples of both true romance and the devastation of sin upon future events. Yet even these pale in comparison to the wildest romance story of them all, the story of Esther.

A peasant and a king! Perhaps this is a parallel to Solomon's Song of Songs, a biblical poem describing how a king is smitten by a beautiful Shulamite woman. (Many Christian scholars and leaders believe it also portrays in prophetic portraiture the fervent love of the King of Kings for His bride.)

In any case, Esther's story is more than a romantic epic. Esther is a spiritual tale of destiny that can help us today: *Preparation and transformation lead to elevation and a passage to purpose.*

Just imagine the transformation required for this young Jewish woman entering the power center of the Persian empire.

INCOMPATIBLE WITH
THE KING'S GLORY

The first issue for Esther—and the first issue for any of us who want intimacy with divinity—is our *incompatibility with the glory* of the King.

Where the heavenly King is concerned, this incompatibility is simply rooted in who we are. Our "peasant" best is not suitable for the palace of His presence.

Garments from the rack of self-righteousness can never compare to being clothed with the righteousness of God in Christ. (These costly garments are not available at the discount markets of man. Only one place has the righteous raiment—the "boutique of innocent blood" established at the cross of Christ.)

Esther the peasant was totally incompatible with the wealth and mind-boggling finery of King Xerxes' summer palace in Susa (a city that was in the southwest portion of what is now Iran; Babylon—where Mordecai presumably grew up as a Jewish exile—was located fifty miles south of modern Baghdad in Iraq).

When Alexander the Great, the Grecian warrior, finally conquered Persia and entered Susa (probably a little more than a century after Esther's time), he was dazzled by the nation's wealth and magnificence.

According to the Greek historian Herodotus, Alexander found twelve hundred tons of gold and silver bullion along with 270 tons of minted gold coins that had been accumulated by Persian kings! This was only a fraction of what was there in King Xerxes' day, long before Persia's treasuries were drained by numerous unsuccessful wars and abandoned building projects.[14]

It was into this incredible mix of absolute power, international politics, and unimaginable wealth that the young Jewish peasant girl named Hadassah (or "Esther," as she would become) entered with destiny at her heels. To put it kindly, no matter *how refined* Hadassah may have been, it wasn't even close to the level expected and *demanded* by the king of Persia and his attendants.

The Scriptures do not explicitly say that Esther was a farm girl, but for the sake of illustration, we might say that to the servants and officers of King Xerxes' court, Esther stepped into the palace smelling as if she was fresh from the barn and not too fond of baths.

ESTHER'S BEST
WASN'T GOOD ENOUGH

Esther was just not acceptable as she was. This is not because she was unclean or smelled badly, but simply because *her best wasn't good enough* for the king. It was the same for *every* candidate preparing for her one night with the king. In order to enter the rarified atmosphere of the palace, you must smell "heavenly"! You just couldn't smell earthy.

> Then the king's servants who attended him said: "Let beautiful young virgins be sought for the king; and let the king appoint officers in all the provinces of his kingdom, that they may gather all the beautiful young virgins to Shushan [Susa] the citadel, into the women's quarters, under the custody of Hegai the king's eunuch, custodian of the women. And let beauty preparations be given *them*. Then let the young woman who pleases the king be queen instead of Vashti." This thing pleased the king, and he did so.[15]

It seems so simple—"And let beauty preparations be given them." While this might be a short sentence, don't let that fool you. Further reading into the biblical account will tell you that this "beauty preparation" took twelve months!

How long do we spend in "beauty preparations" for our encounters with our King? Do you really understand that Esther spent twelve months (that is *twelve* months) of intense effort to prepare for one night? Remember, one year preparing for one night! How, or more appropriately, *why* do you spend twelve months preparing for one encounter?

THE BRIDE WAS BEAUTIFULLY ARRAYED....

While walking through a hotel lobby located on a beautiful Caribbean island nation where I was to minister one evening, I saw an outdoor wedding taking place in that incredible tropical setting. The bride was beautifully arrayed in a brilliant white dress, with carefully chosen jewelry and adornments. Every hair was beautifully arranged in its proper place despite the steady tropical breeze.

It was *her* day, and everyone in the large wedding party knew it—especially her impeccably dressed groom. I have never experienced the joys and struggles of being a bride, but I am happy to say I've experienced the joy of being a groom for the wife of my youth. All I know about a bride's experiences is what I've learned from my wife and the anticipation that comes from having three daughters. In fact, in some measure *they* have already begun the planning and preparation required for their wedding day.

If you have been a bride, then you could outline in great detail just how long it took you to prepare for that one special day, the day that would set the stage for the rest of your life. I'm fairly confident that you didn't just get up one morning and say, "I'll take a shower and grab something from the closet! I think I'll have it all ready this afternoon."

Am I correct, or is all of this a myth? The power and value of the wedding day in a woman's heart has everything to do with the preparation that goes into it—regardless of the budget involved. Whether a woman makes her own dress, has her mother's wedding dress altered, or purchases a dress from an expensive bridal boutique—it must be the *right* dress.

IT COSTS YOU SOMETHING TO PREPARE

Even the pressure of proper protocol and acceptable etiquette weighs in on the blushing bride. Everyone in the wedding party (whether it is simply a lone bridesmaid with the teary dad or a small army of forty participants) must be lined up in order, on time, and wearing the proper wedding clothes. If the rehearsal doesn't sap your strength, then the reception probably will! *It costs you something to prepare for the single most significant day and night of your life.* (If you don't make it past the rehearsal, you may not make it for the wedding!)

The Bible says that Esther spent twelve months preparing for one night with the king in some unique ways:

> Each young woman's turn came to go in to King [Xerxes] *after she had completed twelve months' preparation, according to the regulations for the women,* for thus were the days of their preparation apportioned: *six months with oil of myrrh,* and *six months with perfumes* and *preparations for beautifying women.*[16]

Most of us want to skip past the minor details of these passages, but perhaps there's an apothecary's lesson to be learned here. "Dead flies cause the ointment of the apothecary to send forth a stinking savour."[17] Flies in the ointment of preparation in weddings or worship can create disastrous results in the court of the king. Beelzebub—lord of the flies—will always try to sour the oil of anointing.[18]

Esther spent the first six months of her stay in the palace undergoing "preparations" utilizing oil of myrrh. The second six months seemed to follow the same procedures, but using perfumes (or sweet spices).

YOU BUY A BOTTLE AND SPLASH IT ON—RIGHT?

We have a serious handicap when trying to understand the importance of preparation when going before a Middle-Eastern ruler. Most Western Christians grew up illiterate in the protocol of perfume in Middle-Eastern cultures. We just don't understand all of the focus on fragrance. You buy a bottle, splash it on, and go on your way. Right?

During a recent trip to the United Kingdom, my hosts placed me in a very nice London hotel, which seemed to be very full. I know this because I was moved to another room to accommodate some guests who had made prior arrangements.

It turned out that the hotel was filled with Saudi Arabian and Kuwaiti guests who had come there for some type of gathering. To be honest, I felt as if I was a stranger who had wandered into an exclusive Middle-Eastern hotel. Everywhere you looked, there were guests with flowing robes accompanied by veiled women and a whole entourage of family, staff, and hotel service personnel.

It was a unique experience just to walk down the halls of that place. Old hotels—even exclusive hotels of the exotic variety—often smell a little musty and moldy. Not *this* one. It smelled wonderful! The only way I can describe it is to say that the entire place was inundated with the sweet fragrance of exotic flowers. It was incredible!

When I stepped into a hotel elevator to go to my room, the full power of the fragrance instantly flooded my senses. That was when I realized it wasn't the hotel itself that smelled so good.

The elevator was already occupied by two veiled Middle-Eastern ladies and their husbands. *They* were the source of the indescribable fragrance. When the veiled and robed guests stepped off the elevator, I turned to a hotel staff member (who remained on the elevator with me) and commented about the aroma. (I couldn't help but satisfy my curiosity):

"That smells incredible."

She replied, "You should see inside their rooms!"

"What do you mean?"

"They bring the fragrances from the Middle East to their rooms," she said. "The women lay out their clothes on a little latticework device before they wear them. They light trays of fragrant incense burners underneath the latticework frames so the fragrance saturates their clothes while they bathe or tend to other duties."

It's no wonder that the wonderful fragrance of the incense permeated the hallways, lobby, and elevators of the building! The fragrance simply goes with its bearers. This modern example sets us up to better understand the role played by fragrances and incense in the harems and bridal preparations for ancient Middle-Eastern kingdoms.

THE FRAGRANCE SATURATES THEIR SKIN AND CLOTHING

It has long been known that fragrant oils and spices were major exports of Persia. What is little known is how these fragrances and spices were used by the residents from antiquity. We already know it was common for spices to be burned in religious rituals. However, it also appears that Persian women placed, in small cosmetic burners, the oils of roses and cloves and the essence of musk on coals to perfume their skin and clothing.

They did it by "crouching naked" over a cosmetic burner with a robe draped over them like a tent, essentially forming a personal fragrance sauna.[19] It is my suspicion that Esther learned these Persian beauty secrets from Hegai (the king's chamberlain) and from her own servants. (It seems Middle-Eastern culture was virtually the birthplace of perfumery.)

MYRRH IS A *BITTER* HERB
WITH A SWEET SMELL

The Bible says Esther spent the first six months of her stay in the king's palace being prepared with a *regimen using oil of myrrh*. Myrrh is the fragrant resinous gum of a plant with astringent properties (meaning that it naturally constricts soft [organic] tissue and restricts the flow of bodily fluids). It is considered a *bitter herb*, but it was often combined with the sweeter fragrance of frankincense in various formulas.

Myrrh was included in the two holy preparations used in the worship and ministry to God in the tabernacle of Moses. It was used in both the *holy anointing oil* and in the thicker mixture burned before the Lord as *holy incense*. Both preparations were considered so sacred and holy (as set apart exclusively for God) that anyone who used them for personal or profane (common) use faced the death penalty.

It is remarkable that myrrh appears at least five times in the life of Jesus.

First, at His birth, wise men from the East, who came to offer gifts to the newborn King of the Jews, brought Him precious myrrh.[20]

Second, at Jesus' first anointing, the unnamed "sinful woman" used *muron,* a distilled and costly form of myrrh in droplet or ointment form, to *anoint* Jesus' feet along with her tears in the house of Simon the Pharisee. (This is one of the purest pictures of the *bitterness* of repentance leading to the *sweetness* of forgiveness and divine acceptance.)[21]

Third, at Jesus' second anointing, Mary, the sister of Martha, anointed Jesus with muron (or myrrh) once again in Bethany, at the house of Simon the Leper, but this time anointed His head. Jesus told the disciples Mary had anointed Him for His burial. Here again, the myrrh served as the anointing oil of *bitterness.*[22]

Fourth, at Jesus' death, myrrh was mixed into a drink by the Roman soldiers and offered to Jesus on the cross just before He died (possibly because of its astringent and medicinal qualities). Myrrh is often linked with repentance and sanctification, or being set apart unto God.

Why did Jesus refuse the drink containing myrrh when He was on the cross? Could it be because His mission was to take sin upon Himself totally—to fully become sin? Repentance would have voided His mission.

As the sacrificed Lamb of God, His purpose was to take the complete pun-
ishment for our sin and to be separated from the Father. This is why He
cried out in the end, "My God, My God, why have You forsaken Me?"[23]

Finally, at Jesus' burial, myrrh was one of the fragrances and spices of
choice used to wrap the Lord's body after His death.[24]

Again, myrrh was a principle ingredient in the holy anointing oil that
was daubed onto priests, instruments, furniture, and other people as an act
of holy sanctification and separation unto God. Myrrh also was burned as
a part of the holy incense formula, used in soaking baths, offered in drinks
for internal cleansing, and even eaten for purification purposes.

This fragrance was to be woven throughout the life of Jesus, from His
birth to His burial—even gracing the tomb of His resurrection from the
dead! So should the fragrance of repentance and purity be woven into every
aspect of our lives. The parallels of Esther's preparation to our Lord's progression to the "cross of destiny" are astounding.[25] The spiritual application
almost seems to be that the fragrance of anointing is not optional. You must
have myrrh!

ESTHER LITERALLY "OOZED" FRAGRANCE

The first six months of Esther's preparation speak of cleansing, purification, and the removal of all toxins and defiling agents, both within and
without. The constant bathing and application with oil of myrrh cleansed,
purified, and softened the skin. It also embedded the fragrance deeply. In
other words, Esther literally "oozed" fragrance.

If we want to live in God's presence, we must make repentance a part
of our daily and moment-by-moment routine. We should breathe it in and
pray it out, rub it deep into our being to remove impurities and soften our
hardened attitudes, and ingest it to cleanse our inward parts.

The role of myrrh in the Old Testament sacrifices and in Jesus' life,
death, and burial paints a vivid picture of killing the old man, removing
the blemishes, purging the inner recesses, and turning away from old prac-
tices, habits, mindsets, and limitations. It speaks of change, cleansing, and
sanctification in preparation for an appearance before the King of Kings.

Esther followed the half year of cleansing and purification (with myrrh) with *another* intensive six-month period of immersion and saturation with "sweet spices." It almost certainly included *frankincense* and also perhaps onchya, stacte, galbanum, cassia, and cinnamon.

Worship covers us with the fragrance of the King! In fact, the real purpose of soaking in the oil of anointing (repentance) is to camouflage any smell of the flesh. It is what allows the King to stand to be in the same room with us!

Unlike myrrh, *frankincense only releases its fragrance in the heat of a fire.* It was used (along with the other specified ingredients) in the preparation of both the sacred anointing oil for kings and priests and for the incense burned as a sacrifice to God in the Jewish temple.

> Sometimes worship releases its sweetest fragrance when offered from the fires of trial and adversity.

Some forms of worship only release their sweetest fragrance to God when offered from the fires of trials and adversity. The sacrifice of praise offered in times of trouble is especially sweet and pleasant to the King of Kings. This is worship from a posture of trust and faith instead of suspicion and doubt.

In the tabernacle and temple of ancient Israel, the smoke of this holy incense wafted past the veil of separation as a praise offering of sweetness to Jehovah God, and it obscured from view the "flesh" of the ministering priests.

This speaks of the return of pure praise and worship to the place of prominence once seen in the tabernacle of David and in the temple of Solomon. Our sinful flesh is covered by the blood of the Lamb and by the sweet-smelling cloud of our worship filling the room. This is where God's presence descends in response to a pleasing sacrifice.

Esther began as an orphaned peasant, but through her perseverance in preparation, her unequalled beauty in ministry to the king, and her submission in intercession, she orchestrated the deliverance of an entire nation.

Never underestimate the potential of one service. *Never underestimate the potential of one encounter.* Never underestimate the potential of one woman or man. Don't short-circuit the preparation process. Soak in the oil! Mix in the myrrh of repentance and cleansing! Immerse yourself without inhibitions in the sweet odors of worship, adoration, and lingering ministry to God.

Who knows—the deliverance of your family, your church, or your nation may come about because of one night with the King!

Finding favor with the King can alter your destiny. Never underestimate what one night in the King's presence can do. One night with the King changes everything!

> PROTOCOL *of the* PALACE
>
> 1. Never underestimate the potential of one encounter.

Even thirty seconds in the manifest presence of God can change your future. Esther had a blind date with destiny, and so do you!

Sometimes you just need a lengthy "soaking" in the holy anointing oil to prepare you for your divine appointment. You have a destiny-altering date with the King!

CHAPTER 2

THE KING OR THE KINGDOM?

The Palace or His Presence?

Money, fame, and fear can motivate people to do some crazy things. They also share a sad legacy with another motivator in human history, called "lust." Some people would sell their mothers or their children to gain financial security. Others would sacrifice their reputation and every ounce of their self-esteem for one minute in the national spotlight or a few moments of stolen pleasures in another person's bed. I know of one man who even gave up a lifetime inheritance for a bowl of beans.

> Whatever impresses you attracts you. Whatever you pursue becomes your purpose.

Whatever impresses you attracts you. Whatever you pursue becomes your purpose. What are you pursuing—the King or the kingdom?

It stands to reason that most of the young maidens ushered into this ancient world's most important beauty contest would be enamored with the king's palace. Most people would find it hard to blame them.

The city of Susa was home to the summer capital of Persia under King Xerxes' family line. The Bible gives us a detailed snapshot of the courtyard in the palace garden.

> The courtyard was decorated with beautifully woven *white and blue linen hangings,* fastened by *purple ribbons to silver rings* embedded in *marble pillars. Gold and silver couches* stood on a *mosaic pavement* of porphyry [rock composed of feldspar crystals embedded in a dark red or purple groundmass, "red marble"],[1] marble, mother-of-pearl, and other costly stones. Drinks were served in

gold goblets of many designs, and there was an abundance of royal wine, just as the king had commanded.[2]

If this is merely a description of the king's "backyard patio," can you imagine how his throne room and palace looked? Today far too many Christians are enamored with the finite finery and earthly benefits of God's kingdom rather than its King. Whether we look at people in the palace of King Xerxes of ancient Persia or those attending church services in contemporary culture, far too many of us tend to be so taken with the glamour of a mansion that we ignore the man behind the mansion. We neglect the face behind the place.

In society some people are drawn to the power and prestige of the "throne." They devote their energies toward receiving every gift possible from the hands of the one in power. The slogan on both sides of the equation might read: "Take what *they* have before they take what *you* have."

Often we don't do much better in the church. How frequently do we bounce back and forth between treating God as a loving Father one moment (which is good) and as the Supreme Slot Machine the rest of the time (which is not good)?

PLUGGING COINS INTO THE SPIRITUAL SLOT MACHINE

We "go at prayer" as if we are plugging coins into the Supreme Slot Machine, hoping He will spit out winnings to us—while at the same time we are envious of the rest of the spiritual gamblers and their "gifts."

We have no reason or need to justify the actions and morals of the historical King Xerxes. He wasn't Christian, he wasn't Jewish, and he wasn't even "nice" by any stretch of the imagination. He was a cruel and powerful ruler in a brutal and violent age. Nevertheless, this Persian king represented in some respects the eternal worth of the great King of Kings (*in allegory*).

King Xerxes must have seen every kind of pandering diplomat, whining politician, and subservient prince pass through his throne room. It is safe to assume they left mountains of self-serving gifts in his treasury at Susa. Even the ancient pagan world understood what few in our culture have grasped: *You never come before a king empty-handed. You always bring a gift.* In fact, your "gift" will make room for you![3]

The great King of Kings and Lord of Lords has seen an unending parade of people attempt to attract His attention or impress Him since time began. Most were dressed in the rags of their own efforts at holiness. Some entered His gates robed in various levels of thanksgiving, and precious few came enveloped in worship.

In my mind, I often imagine Him saying to Himself, "Who will love *Me* more than the things I can give them? Where are the people who are more interested in touching *My heart* than in sampling My splendor?"

King Solomon must have wrestled with the same problem throughout his reign. He got off to a good start, but his God-given gifts elevated him so high in the eyes of others that he was lifted up in his own eyes. (Evidently he didn't do a very good job of redirecting the praise back to God. It seems he began to "believe his own press.")

Long before Xerxes developed his harem, Solomon began to focus less on God and more on his own personal lusts and desires. Eventually Solomon must have believed that he was too wise to fail or fall, because he set aside the direct command of God and gave his heart to foreign women who served demonic idols. He accumulated a staggering seven hundred wives and royal mistresses and three hundred additional concubines or secondary wives (most of them from forbidden nations serving false gods).[4]

In the end God seemed to step out of the picture, and He allowed Solomon to carry on the show in his own wisdom. The spotlight of the nation turned away from the glory of the One in the temple to the glory of the gifted man on the earthly throne.

Once Solomon was seen as the primary source of wealth and promotion, the king's favor began to carry more weight than God's favor. Solomon inadvertently became the nation's god and idol.

HOW DO YOU ATTRACT A MAN WITH A THOUSAND WIVES?

Carrying the full weight of his celebrity status, a disguised King Solomon falls in love with a nameless shepherdess called "the Shulamite." Some of the most romantic prose ever written dripped from the pen of the wisest man who ever lived—he wrote the Song of Solomon about his overwhelming attraction to this peasant girl!

Why would a famous ruler with a thousand wives become so intrigued with a simple commoner? He did it for the same reasons King Xerxes fell for Esther. Both leaders had their pick of the most beautiful women in the known world. Perhaps each ruler was fascinated that a beautiful young maiden might fall in love with *him* rather than with his regal power and authority as a great king.

It seems that royalty must always carry the baggage of doubt. Sheer survival forces them to be skeptical that people could or would ever love them for something *other* than personal gain or elevated position.

Although we would never call the Almighty One skeptical, it is safe to say He dearly longs for more followers who, like Esther, will fall in love with the King rather than the King's blessings. I know God's heart desires those who love the *Giver* more than the gift!

It was Jesus who told us that His Father constantly searches for certain people in the earth. I am not saying that God is a respecter of persons, but He does seem to have *wants*, in the sense that He "wants" us to worship Him in spirit and in truth: "The Father is looking for anyone who will worship him that way."[5]

Some may feel differently about Esther than I do, but I am convinced that God somehow anointed and prepared this young orphaned Jewish maiden from childhood to see *something* worthy of love in the seemingly pernicious King Xerxes.

> PROTOCOL *of the* PALACE
> 2. Seek the heart of the King, not the splendor of His kingdom.

Somehow, in some way, God *anointed and appointed* that young woman to stand out from all of the rest of the beautiful women in that expansive Persian harem. God prepared and equipped Esther to soften—and win—the heart of the strongest dictator of her day.

Esther didn't realize that the very lives of her people would depend on what happened during her first encounter with the king. I believe *the secret to Esther's success was a God-given desire to seek the heart of the king rather than the splendor of his kingdom.*

JESUS, ON THE CROSS, TOOK THE ROLE OF ESTHER

Let me share yet another strange twist of analogy on the divine purpose. Do you realize that Jesus symbolically took on the *role of Esther* in His ministry? That He willingly gave Himself to the cruel earthly "king," called Death, and allowed His body to be laid on the "bed of death" in another man's tomb?

God never misses the opportunity to put His signature upon significant events in human history. Jesus fully surrendered His virgin flesh and spotless soul to *death* on a cross in order to free us from its ultimate control forever.

Esther obviously had a divine appointment with destiny, but how did she move from one among hundreds in the king's harem to number one in the king's heart? It seems to me that God caused something unique to happen within Esther. It is as if she was groomed from birth for "such a time as this."

AN UNSEEN HAND MOVED ASIDE EVERY OBSTACLE

There seemed to be a supernatural love and aura about her that won extreme loyalty and favor from people in positions of power—including her enemies! It was as if an unseen hand moved aside every obstacle to strategically advance and position her.

Some people want to reject the book of Esther out of hand, asking, "Why would God cause Esther to lose her virginity in the bed of an uncircumcised (Persian) Gentile?" I don't know the answer fully because I am not God, so I seek the answer from something I *do* know from God's Word.

I ask a similar question with even *higher* stakes: "Why would God cause

His own Son to die on the cross of uncircumcised Gentile (Roman) soldiers at the demand of circumcised Jewish priests?"

We *do* know the answer to that question. Isn't it written somewhere that "God *so loved the world* that he gave his only Son, so that everyone who believes in him will not perish but have eternal life"?[6]

Whether it is in a Persian king's bedroom or on a cruel Roman cross, *you can find God in some of the most interesting places.* And you can work God's will in some of the strangest responses. One writer put it in this manner in the Bible: "Truly, O God of Israel, our Savior, *you work in strange and mysterious ways.*"[7]

Most of the prejudice against the book of Esther stems from misunderstandings over such "mysterious ways." Many people find it hard to justify God's plans and methods in Esther's life because they assume that all the books in the Bible are identical in style and purpose.

They aren't.

The apostle Paul encouraged us to "be diligent to present yourself approved to God as a workman who does not need to be ashamed, accurately handling the word of truth."[8] People who *have* studied the Scriptures extensively will tell you that the only way to accurately study the book of Esther is to understand the nature of "Hebrew narrative," the literary form used in this case. Hebrew narrative is not *overt* teaching but *covert;* it does not spell out the motives and inner thoughts of the characters—*these are revealed through action and speech.* It is up to the reader to draw his or her own conclusions.[9] Now let's throw back the cover!

XERXES WAS HANDSOME, AMBITIOUS, RUTHLESS, AND JEALOUS

The aforementioned ancient Greek historian Herodotus characterized Xerxes as one of the three most formidable Persian kings ever. He also described him as the tallest and most handsome of them all, an ambitious and ruthless ruler, a brilliant warrior, and a jealous lover.[10]

The attributes of attractiveness, ambition, ruthlessness, and jealousy didn't stop with the throne room. The same spirit of conquest and competition must have permeated every square inch of the women's quarters.

It doesn't take much imagination to picture the competitive spirit that must have been rife in the king's harem. Be sure of this—these women weren't spending a year cultivating great character! Can you imagine the scene? Streams of curtained litters bearing the finalists, each young woman hoping with all her heart to have her place in the sun? Imagine the petty rivalries, the infighting, the envy, and the jealousy. Imagine how tough it would be to maintain spiritual equilibrium when everything and everyone around you is emphasizing only the condition and shape of your body and the beauty of your face![11]

ESTHER WAS THROWN INTO A SCHOOL OF SEDUCTION

It was into this frenzied "school of seduction" that the lovely Esther was gently but *permanently* placed. The outlook was grim. There was no escape from the splendor of the king's quarters for women. No matter what happened in the years ahead, each of the women in that place were his property.

Whether they saw him once and were forgotten (which is possibly exactly what happened to all but *one* of the women) or went on to become Xerxes' queen, they would never return to their families, they would never realize their childhood dreams—they would never even walk the familiar streets of the city as they once did. After an encounter with the king, they would never be the same.

I suppose something similar happens to the family members of presidents and prime ministers. They have to adjust to having a retinue of Secret Service agents and security officers following them around (and dictating most of their moves) all of the time. They can't even go to the bathroom without someone noticing and radioing the exciting news to somebody else.

Esther was surrounded by glamour and luxury, but she was *not* in a comfortable place. Chuck Swindoll said:

> This was the place to get high on seduction. This is the place where women cultivated the ability to use their charm to get what they wanted—namely, the highest office a woman could hold in

the kingdom. This was the place where women had available to them all the jewelry, all the perfume, all the cosmetics, all the clothing needed to make them physically attractive and alluring to the lonely king. This was the place that would make Nordstrom and Tiffany, Saks Fifth Avenue and Neiman Marcus fade into insignificance.

Yet it is in this heady environment that Esther, God's lovely star, shines the brightest.[12]

EVERY REASON *NOT* TO FALL IN LOVE WITH XERXES

To make matters worse than they already were, Esther had every reason *not* to fall in love with the king of the Persians. She was Jewish; Xerxes was not. Her parents had died under the domination of Persia. We know they were included among and/or descended from the Jews who had been transported to Babylon under King Nebuchadnezzar and then were forced to adapt when Persia's King Cyrus conquered the Babylonians.

No one but God knows for certain, but it is possible that Esther's parents died due to a tragedy in Babylon—it is relatively rare for *both* parents of a young child to die of natural causes. Regardless of the circumstances, we know that an older cousin named Mordecai took in the young orphan named Hadassah. Mordecai lived in Susa and served King Xerxes as a royal scribe.

Esther knew what it was to live at risk. She was a Jew and an orphan in the capital city of a violent and pagan world-empire. Now she had been "drafted," separated from the only family she had ever known, and thrown into a dog-eat-dog beauty pageant.

The entry fee for all of the entrants was one night with the king of the most feared nation on earth (again, scholars estimate there were from 400 to 1,460 women in the contest).

LIFE AT THE TOP OF THE PERSIAN FOOD CHAIN

The grand prize was an all-expenses-paid life at the top of the empire's "food chain" as the queen of Persia. Since Esther had spent many years growing up in Susa, we have to believe that she thoroughly understood what it meant to be the bride of the king. I'm convinced Esther sensed destiny at work in her life, even if she didn't grasp (or understand) the details.

Esther must have known that as queen she would enjoy a certain level of access to virtually anything the king had access to. I imagine Esther thinking to herself, *If I win the heart of the king, if the king favors me, then I don't have to worry about jewelry, clothing, or my family's safety for the rest of my life. The king will always provide for his queen.*

Perhaps she understood that one day of favor can be worth more than a lifetime of labor!

> PROTOCOL *of the* PALACE
>
> 3. One day of favor can be worth more than a lifetime of labor!

We tend to focus on our particular crises and personal needs exclusively, while God orchestrates the destinies of billions—and He does it in perfect harmony with His purpose for humanity over the entire span of time.

For Esther, the miracle began when she chose to seek the *heart* of the *king* rather than merely the *splendor* of the kingdom. Esther likely had no idea that she would spend an entire year *preparing* for one night with the king and that she could possibly *wait* another four years before it was her turn to go into his bedchambers.

I'm convinced that Esther's commitment to love set up a transformation in the king's heart. Suddenly he found himself looking at her differently than he did all the other young virgins who had come before him. Something elevated her from a mere object of his *lust* to the object of his *love*.

Mere physical attraction and sexual prowess could not have been the key. God was about to transcend normal procedures and arrange a "marriage of state" between His daughter and the son of His chosen vessel, Darius.[13] He carefully equipped and positioned Esther for the task from birth.

Perhaps He permitted Esther to see past the hard face and emotional scars of the ruthless warrior and to look beyond the casual attention of the royal womanizer. There is a possibility that Esther's divinely anointed demeanor disarmed Xerxes, allowing him to reveal his vulnerability.

It seems that Esther saw something through a divine window that activated her heart and helped her to win the king's. It was her destiny in God.

Some maintain that King Xerxes married Esther strictly for her stunning good looks (and perhaps because of whatever happened during her first night with him). Even *if* King Xerxes had married Esther for her appearance, he kept her because of her heart.

> You are chosen for potential but kept because of passion.

In the palace of the heavenly King, *you are chosen for potential but kept because of passion.* He knows the potential He created you to fulfill, but He keeps you close because He loved you enough to give Himself for you.

We will leave the mystery of intimacy to just that, a mystery—nevertheless, this story should be a revelation to us of how the hand of God operates in "non-religious" matters.

PROTOCOL OF HIS PRESENCE

The story of Esther is a revelation about a peasant who becomes educated in the protocol of the king's presence. I believe she fell in love with the king, while all the other young girls fell in love with the palace, the prestige, the food, and the opulent luxury of their surroundings.

Consumers eat at the King's table with only the occasional obligatory nod toward the King Himself. Consuming His blessings, they love His *gifts*—His power, His provision—but do they love *Him*? On the other hand, *worshipers* nibble at the same table, totally focused on the *King*.

To put things in simpler terms, Esther realized that *without the king, the king's palace*—as nice and as legendary as it was—*was just a big empty house.*

(Many people know this to be true about their local church: If God isn't there, it's just a big empty building.)

Esther probably knew hundreds of concubines who lived in the palace with her, but they didn't have the king. They were merely recipients of a luxurious lifestyle. So Esther made the conscious decision not to merely go after the *palace* lifestyle—she would go for the *princess lifestyle*. She was the girl who would be queen. She would love the king!

> The King's palace without the King is just a big empty house.

There may be hundreds of "spiritual concubines" around you day after day and year after year, people who have moved in to stay after one life-changing encounter with God yet have failed to seek His heart, preferring instead to content themselves with the benefits of lounging around in His house!

We must make the decision not to settle for the church-palace lifestyle of pleasing self. We must go for the princess lifestyle and seek to please the King.

It is time for us to be the church who would be queen, the bride of Christ.

Concubines may have had an *experience* with the King. His bride would *have* the King!

CHAPTER 3

PROTOCOL OF THE PALACE

*You Cannot Worship
What You Dethrone*

E very palace has its protocol, and every executive residence has its formal rules of conduct. A palace protocol is "a code prescribing strict adherence to correct etiquette and precedence."[1] Buckingham Palace, in London, has a time-honored protocol, and so do the White House in Washington and the Kremlin in Moscow. The higher and greater the authority of the king or leader, the more detailed and rigid the protocol.

Some who come to a king's front gate are merely *onetime visitors* seeking a onetime audience. These temporary travelers master only the most basic procedures of protocol, and they are only allowed to visit the outer courts of the royal palace. They access only those places where the simple, learned behaviors of protocol suffice—the things common to virtually everyone, even outside the palace. To this day young ladies who may never grace Buckingham Palace are taught to curtsy, and young men who have never seen royalty still know how to bow.

A second group, one that might be called *guests of the king,* comes for official business of a more extended nature. Of necessity, these individuals must master much more of the protocol of the palace. The things they seek and the requests they make take place only in the deeper regions of the royal residence, behind more private doors and in more privileged places (protected by more layers of security).

Then there are the *intimates,* those who have made life in the ruler's court their primary focus. These are rare individuals, few in number, but great in privileged access. They understand how to treat a king or queen with the proper respect and honor due their royal status. These select few know how to approach a monarch because they thoroughly comprehend and follow the protocol of the palace.

With only a handful of monarchies remaining in the modern world, it seems that very few of us understand how to approach the emperor of Japan or the queen of England. We know the basic formalities we likely learned as children—the curtsy and the bow—but beyond these simple courtesies, we feel lost. More prominent deference to royalty seems to be a forgotten skill—we display an evident casualness fostered by the equalizing nature of modern political movements and individual rights.

We find ourselves awkward and poorly equipped, needing to regain the long-lost art of elevating a monarch and magnifying a king. Even the language of honor seems foreign to us. How many of us have read words of Scripture placed in royal settings and wondered about the culture that birthed them? What was going through Isaiah's head when he wrote, in prophetic power of Lucifer's forbidden royal ambition, "I will ascend into heaven, I will exalt my throne above the stars of God"?[2] You cannot worship what you dethrone!

The jealousy of human nature tends to tear down, but worship builds up. Even the Son of God collided with this wall of negativity. Jesus visited His hometown but was limited to performing only a few minor miracles there due to the pervasive unbelief and casual familiarity.

> You cannot worship what you dethrone!

The people of Nazareth could not or would not honor Jesus for who He was—they insisted on trying to pull Him back down to His childhood level so that they could make Him their equal. The problem is that He *was* the King, a ruler without precedent or equal. Jesus said, "Only in his hometown, among his relatives and in his own house is a prophet without honor."[3]

The court protocol of King Xerxes focused on extreme security for the world's most feared and powerful monarch, and it created an imposing presentation for the world's richest and mightiest king.

Protocol was especially important in Persia's royal courts. An atmosphere of distrust dominated every palace and royal city in use by King Xerxes, particularly due to the unpleasant tendency of Persian kings to be assassinated by their own family members and trusted counselors.[4]

The Persian kingdom under Xerxes stretched from India to Ethiopia, ruling over twenty-three nations on as many as three continents. Persian protocol required the kings of defeated or subservient countries to humble themselves in a grand procession, carrying their tribute money from one royal building to another, past scores of tall colonnades, until they finally bowed before King Xerxes himself in the royal throne room.

PROTOCOL *of the* PALACE

4. Worship is the protocol that protects the King and qualifies the visitor.

The palace protocol helped weed out unimportant, less worthy, or inappropriate petitions, requests, and complaints. Most could be diverted to lesser officials. Throughout the procession that brought them to the throne room, the king's wealth, power, and absolute authority over the lives of his subjects overwhelmed would-be visitors. *The elaborate protocol was meant to protect the king and qualify the visitor.* By the time people actually made it into King Xerxes' throne room, they knew they were in the presence of a powerful ruler.

Part of the lesson of protocol is the importance of *waiting.* How much time have you spent waiting? We willingly bide our time at the doctor's office; we've read every dog-eared magazine and children's Bible at the orthodontist's office; we can tell you how many light fixtures flicker at our state's Department of Transportation licensing office; and we even pay exorbitant fees to stand in line at our favorite theme parks during the hottest season of the year. Yet we consider these to be irritating exceptions to the ironclad rule: We want what we want, and we want it *now*!

We live in a culture of instant gratification, and there is no greater enemy to intimacy. (Many today don't even "wait" for marriage to become intimate!)

If someone is truly important, they are worth the wait. Often people would wait for days or weeks to have an appointment with the king. Others today refuse to wait and instead forge ahead, with their petitions ignored or their destiny deterred. We only wait for what we value. When it is all said and done, *waiting is worship.*

If you chose to ignore the protocol of an ancient king (or of a modern leader for that matter), you would be listed as *persona non grata*,[5] and your palace passport would be stamped "ACCESS DENIED." In extreme cases, you could even be executed for "rushing" the throne.

THE MASTER OF THE ROYAL AUDIENCES

Any visitor seeking to approach the throne of Persia, who actually made it through all the gates, would in the end have to contend with a powerful warrior/official who commanded the king's personal thousand-man bodyguard. This "master of the royal audiences" was usually a war hero and champion warrior who was greatly trusted by the king. He occupied "the one office which could outweigh all others in power and influence" (other than the king himself), and he personally controlled *who* was able to see the king and *when.*[6] (Then, too, you would meet this imposing figure only after having mastered the art of palace protocol.)

To some people outside the kingdom of God, the brand of Christianity they see on certain television shows and at the neighborhood church on the corner must appear just as layered and protected as the Persian court. Too often they see preachers and priests as the "masters of the royal audiences," passing judgment on who gets in and who doesn't. (Jesus is the real "Door," the Master of the Audiences for all who would see the Father in heaven.)

Since most unsaved people *know* they aren't holy, all too often they just give up and "leave religion to the righteous folks." Christianity can appear to be a maze of walls—walls of good works, of dress codes, of "secret handshakes," and of special religious lingo—designed to keep the uninitiated away from a secretive God.

But there is a roadmap to God's presence . . . and love stamps your visa.

With the rise of the personal computer, video games, and the Internet, we have seen an incredible explosion of computer gaming. With much of it based on New Age imagery or overtly occultic sources, millions of people find themselves mesmerized for hours at a time as they try to find their way through myriad mazes, playing fictitious roles in imaginary worlds.

The goal is to progress from one level of intimacy and power to the next. (I don't promote these fictitious games; I am fully engaged with the real King, in whose presence I find all that I need.) What amazes me is the amount of energy some will expend in an imaginary world, only to ignore the spiritual world!

Nevertheless, the quest for access in such popular games seems similar to the maze that confronted people wanting to see the king of Persia. The Greek philosopher Aristotle described the Persian court in a letter to his student Alexander the Great:

> The pomp of Cambyses and Xerxes and Darius was ordered on a grand scale and touched the heights of majesty and magnificence. The King himself, they say, lived in Susa or Exbatana, *invisible to all,* in a marvelous palace with a surrounding wall flashing with gold, electrum and ivory; it had a succession of many gate-towers, and the gateways, separated by many stades[7] from one another, were fortified with brazen doors and high walls.
>
> Outside these the leaders and most eminent men were drawn up in order, some as personal bodyguards and attendants to the King himself, some as guardians of each outer wall, called Guards and the Listening-Watch, so that the King himself, who had the name of Master and God, might see everything and hear everything. Apart from these there were others appointed as revenue officials, leaders in war and in the hunt, receivers of gifts to the King, and others, each responsible for administering a particular task, as they were necessary.[8]

THE ESTHER TRANSFORMATION— ONE DAY AT A TIME

In parallel, the truth is that *none of us* deserves to get in, but God Himself has made a way. The Good News is that *all* may come to God at any time if they admit their wrongdoing and surrender their heart to Jesus Christ. (In that instant, God *adopts* them through His Son into His royal family and begins to complete the work of the "Esther transformation" one day at a time. Unfortunately, we often feel overwhelmed by the weight of religious protocol, even *after* we receive Jesus Christ as Lord and Savior.)

It probably seemed impossible for the average Persian citizen to enter the royal residence and fortress in King Xerxes' time. In the same way, it often seems just as impossible for the average Christian to truly come near to or touch the heart of God. Through Jesus Christ, however, the impossible became possible. Even aliens can become intimates. He made a way for us to leave our "former way of life" and to change our thoughts and attitudes. When His protocol is complete in you, you "display a new nature, because you are a new person, created in God's likeness—righteous, holy, and true."[9] This is the transforming miracle of the protocol of His presence.

It wasn't easy to enter the Persian king's presence under normal circumstances. As people approached the king's presence from outside of the royal residence, their first obstacle was the king's gate, an imposing gateway that towered high overhead.

It was impossible to move from *outside* that gate to *inside* the palace courts unless you had the appropriate credentials. It was *designed* that way. How would an average man or woman get their hands on the credentials to pass through such a royal portal? It often took a royal invitation.

FOR ALL THE PEOPLE FROM THE LEAST TO THE GREATEST

There are times in the life of a king when he opens up certain parts of his private inner courts for the public to see:

For a full 180 days [Xerxes] displayed the vast wealth of his kingdom and the splendor and glory of his majesty. *When these days were over, the king gave a banquet, lasting seven days, in the enclosed garden of the king's palace, for all the people from the least to the greatest,* who were in the citadel of Susa. The garden had hangings of white and blue linen, fastened with cords of white linen and purple material to silver rings on marble pillars. There were couches of gold and silver on a mosaic pavement of porphyry, marble, mother-of-pearl and other costly stones. Wine was served in goblets of gold, each one different from the other, and the royal wine was abundant, in keeping with the king's liberality.[10]

The Great King of the church sometimes holds public banquets that allow everyone to witness His glory and celebrate in His joy. We call these times of *revival.* The royal wine of His presence is abundant, and even uninterested non-Christians in the vicinity are caught up in His love and presence.

THE PROTOCOL PATTERN IN THE TABERNACLE OF MOSES

Most of the time, however, we enter the court of the King according to the protocol of His presence. God's Word spelled out a pattern for this protocol in the Old Testament through the tabernacle of Moses. It was a virtual handbook on how to handle the presence of God—how you enter the palace of the King of Kings.

David the psalmist referred to this pattern when he told us, "Enter into His gates with thanksgiving."[11] Thanksgiving *can* be the lowest form of worship because it is dependent on the answer to the question, "What have You done for me lately?" Praise, though, is not dependent on what He has done but on who He is. He is worthy of praise whether you believe He has done anything for you or not!

This first stage of progression in thanksgiving "gets you into the property, on the premises, and under the promises." But there is still more! Then we must enter His inner courts with praise.

There is a difference between thanksgiving and praise. We *thank* God because He has *done something* wonderful in our lives that we want to acknowledge and remember. We *praise* Him because of *who He is,* because of His attributes, or because of His ways. He is worthy of praise—period—whether we are having a good day or a bad day.

PRAISE TAKES YOU INTO HIS COURTS

But there are more rooms in the palace than the outer courts and inner courts. There are also places of intimacy with God. The highest level of praise is worship, and this transports us into the Holy of Holies, the inner chamber, the sacred dwelling place of God's glory.

Worship differs from praise only in the sense that our lives and physical bodies *become* the praise offered to Him. The only thing necessary to qualify you to praise Him is breath. But to truly know Him—that takes worship. This is where we express our love for Him *by bowing* before Him.[11] We humble ourselves before Him simply because of who He is. Worship is not dependent upon what He has done, what He is doing, or upon any other outward circumstance. He is worthy of worship simply because He *is.* This is our unconditional love for our Father in heaven, and this place cannot be entered unless we are "clean" in our hearts and minds with pure motives—loving the Giver more than the gifts. We see a picture of this type of worship in the Revelation of John:

> Day after day and night after night they keep on saying, "Holy, holy, holy is the Lord God Almighty—the one who always was, who is, and who is still to come." Whenever the living beings give glory and honor and thanks to the one sitting on the throne, the one who lives forever and ever, the twenty-four elders *fall down and worship* the one who lives forever and ever. And *they lay their crowns before the throne* and *say,* "You are worthy, O Lord our God, to receive glory and honor and power. For you created everything, and it is for your pleasure that they exist and were created."[13]

The Greek word for "worship" used in this passage is *proskuneo.* It literally means "to kiss, like a dog licking his master's hand; to fawn or crouch to, prostrate oneself in homage (do reverence to, adore): worship."[14] *One's dignity is not preserved in this posture—but the King's majesty is presented!*

THIS IS WORSHIP

The twenty-four elders before the throne of God *worship* Him (even at this very moment!) by falling down before the almighty God. They literally prostrate themselves in humble homage and reverent adoration. Then in willing surrender, over and over again, they lay down the crowns of authority He gave them! They worship Him with the fruit of their lips. *This is worship*—the passionate declaration, demonstration, and celebration of His "worth-ness."

Why does this type of extravagant worship seem so out of place in many churches? Is it that the uninhibited worship is so outlandish, or is it that our understanding, expectations, and standards for true worship are so earthbound and man-centered?

Some of the most treasured "Daddy snapshots" in the memory bank of my mind are of those tender times when my little girls used to climb up in my lap and shower affection upon me. They didn't need a reason. They just did it because they loved their daddy.

I'll never forget the feeling of their soft little curls against my cheek and those tiny arms around my neck. What really melts me is the memory of those big brown eyes staring deeply into mine, followed by the words I'll treasure all of my life: "I wuv you, Daddy."

If I asked in that moment, "What do you want, honey? Do you need anything?" the answer was generally predictable: "No, Daddy. I don't need anything. I just want you."

I don't think my daughters realized it then, but I would have seriously considered emptying my bank account for them in those moments of affection-induced weakness. Unconditional love has a way of making daddies weak in the knees, soft of heart, and liberal with their pocketbook.

There is something special about telling the Father, "No, Daddy. I don't need anything. I just want You." I'm convinced that even our heavenly Father reacts in a special way when we express our love and longing for His presence. Unconditional worship uncovers the King's "weakness" as well!

Adolescence has a way of elevating the impact of peer pressure and inhibiting overt acts of tenderness toward fathers. Don't allow that same syndrome to curtail your displays of worship to your heavenly Father. *Extravagant worship should be the norm, not the exception.*

The King is worthy. Are we simply too intimidated? Jesus said, "Assuredly, I say to you, whoever does not receive the kingdom of God as a little child will by no means enter it."[15]

Right now decide that you are not too old to sit in Daddy's lap. Decide that you will not be intimidated into distancing yourself from Him. The King of Kings said that those who overcome will sit *with* Him on His throne.[16] The protocol of this type of worship is what ushered an uninvited

Mary with an alabaster box into the inner circle. *Go where few dare—into the lap of the King.*

THE INTIMACY OF PASSIONATE WORSHIP

If there is anything that really "speeds up" or bypasses the usual steps of progression in the protocol of His presence, it is this intimacy of passionate worship. Each step is important and valuable, but the earliest steps in the process tend to be the most formal. Especially where prayers of petition are involved.

This was even true in the palace of King Xerxes. All of his subjects had to go through the stiff protocol of the palace to approach him. Even when they made it all the way to His throne, their approach to him was permanently limited by two hip-high pedestal-like incense burners that marked the "Do Not Pass" zone.[17] Anyone who trespassed into this forbidden territory, or even entered the throne room without permission or forgiveness, was immediately executed by large bodyguards holding razor-sharp axes.[18]

> The deeper you go into the palace, the fewer the people.

The protocol of the palace progresses from the front gate all the way to the inner recesses of the king's bedchambers. You will notice that *the deeper you go into the palace, the fewer the people.* The crowd thins out. We see the progression of intimacy even in the public ministry of Jesus to the woman with the chronic hemorrhage.

> *A great multitude* followed Him and *thronged Him.* Now *a certain woman* had a flow of blood for twelve years.[19]

There are three distinct demarcations of intimacy in these passages. There was the multitude, the crowd; then there were those few within the crowd in the immediate vicinity of Jesus, those who "thronged" or compressed Him with their closeness. Finally, there is "a certain woman" who touched Him and tapped the power of intimate faith.

> She came behind Him in the crowd and *touched His garment.* . . . Immediately the fountain of her blood was dried up, and she felt in her body that she was healed of the affliction.[20]

> Position and petition often shout their demands, but passion need only whisper!

It still works the same with King Jesus. The deeper you go into the palace, the fewer the people at that place of access—even in the middle of a crowd. Jesus was surrounded by others, and some were even pushing against Him in the *natural.* Only one touched Him both physically *and* spirit to spirit. You have to do something to stand out.

When you finally get to the bedchambers, you find only the king and his bride. Even the king's most trusted servants are barred from that place of intimacy in private moments.

THE PRINCES OF THE FACE

From the days of Darius forward, there were seven key counselors in the Persian empire who held far greater power and privileges than nearly anyone else. These "princes of the face" could approach the king directly, anytime, day or night, *except* in the royal bedchambers when the king was with a woman.[21] The only other person with equal or greater privileges was the "master of the audiences," mentioned earlier. Then there was also the queen, who, unlike these men, was barred from approaching her husband unannounced but could nevertheless affect destiny from the privacy of the bedchamber. *Position and petition often shout their demands, but passion need only whisper!*

Each of us must individually discover the key of protocol granting access to God's presence. If for some reason you don't, then you might be led to believe that you must *work* or *earn* your way into the King's good graces—even though spiritual DNA tests validate that you are a member of the royal family. You might also believe that only a few really deserving specially chosen or privileged people may actually make it all the way into the magnificent manifest presence of God.

The good news is that there is an even higher "security clearance" available than the protocol of the gates!

Most Christians understand and practice the heavenly protocol of thanksgiving in the outer court, where the efforts of men are made to acknowledge and give thanks to God.

Fewer practice the protocol of praise necessary to enter the holy chamber, where interaction with God is not dependent on the latest list of blessings and gifts they have received from Him.

IS THE REQUIRED BLOODLINE TOO NOBLE?

Only a privileged few are able to move about freely in the royal residence, the Holy of Holies. (In the Old Testament, only priests of the bloodline of Aaron were permitted to venture into the Holy of Holies to minister in God's presence.) This baffles most of the people outside the gates. Secretly, they dream of moving closer to the Great King, but they are sure the cost is too great and the required bloodline too noble for them.

As we have seen, in the kingdom of the Medes and Persians in the fourth century B.C., a strict protocol governed who could approach the king's presence in the royal palace. Yet there was one odd Persian tradition that persisted despite all of the reforms, order, and organization instituted in Persia by Xerxes' father, King Darius.

> "Subjects with a grievance flock[ed] to the King's or governor's gate and ma[de] loud protests. . . ." Historians of the Persian era say this practice was as old as the Achaemenid family line.[22]

I'm convinced this tradition is much older than that! People have been shouting at the heavens and shaking their fists at God since the days of Cain. The line of inappropriate petitioners and indignant complainers outside the gate of worship may be the longest line in human history.

Was it God's intent that we be limited to shouting our demands or requests from outside the court? Absolutely not, but I have to admit that if you scan actual Christian *practice* around the world, you might be convinced this is the case.

What then *is* the protocol that allows access to the presence of God? The Old Testament picture of divine protocol pictures three courts and a priestly progression toward God's shekinah (or visible glory) in the tabernacle of Moses. An eight-foot-high fence established a line of demarcation around the entire tabernacle area, blocking physical access and even the peering eyes of the curious from intruding. (As the Scriptures say, "All have sinned, and come *short.* . . .")[23]

Everyone who entered was to be qualified, and the fence separated all three "courts" of the tabernacle from the invasion of everyday life with only one gate (or opening) leading in.

ENTERING THE EMBASSY OR CONSULATE OF HEAVEN

It was as if the fenced boundaries of the tabernacle marked the sovereign soil of an embassy or consulate of heaven, where God's presence made the very ground holy and set apart. I presume you could shout your petitions and requests loudly from outside, but the only way to properly seek an audience with God was to enter the first gate with an offering in your hand and with the gift of thanksgiving in your heart. This illustrates the dual worship God desires, the worship offered with heart *and* hand, in body *and* in spirit. (It is no accident that we worship Him with lifted hands, humble hearts, illuminated minds, and bent knees.)

Only priests were permitted to enter the court of the Holy Place, where they ministered to the Lord and interceded for humanity together. (This reminds me of a courtroom, where the main things you hear are the formal pleadings and arguments of attorneys petitioning the court and interviewing their clients and witnesses.)

Most of the petitions were offered on the legal basis of God's promises and instructions for the temporary suspension of the penalties of sin or for dedicating certain things and people to God.

The third court was called the Holy of Holies, and it was home to the ark of the covenant. This represented the resident presence of God. It was so holy that only the designated member of Aaron's high-priestly family was permitted to enter it once a year. And *that* only under the cover of a "Holy Smoke" cloud. The smoke created by the smoldering holy incense signified the smoke of praise and worship to God.

> [Aaron the high priest] will fill an incense burner with burning coals from the altar that stands before the LORD. Then, *after filling both his hands with fragrant incense,* he will carry the burner and incense behind the inner curtain. There in the LORD's presence, he will put the incense on the burning coals *so that a cloud of incense will rise over the Ark's cover*—the place of atonement—that rests on the Ark of the Covenant. *If he follows these instructions, he will not die.*[24]

Read that last line again if you think protocol was not important! If there wasn't enough smoke of praise and worship, the high priest just might not return alive from his journey into God's holy presence. Yet it was here that God spoke to man and confirmed His covenant.

Jesus Christ, our high priest, has torn the veil that separates us from God's presence. Now we can enter into His presence through a new and living way (or "protocol")—through the blood of Jesus and through His finished work. In essence, there are more areas in the palace than a courtyard and a courtroom. There is a place of intimacy with God—a behind-the-veil experience.

Petitions presented in the formality of the courtroom may be persuasive, but sometimes a whispered word on the pillow of intimacy can re-direct nations. *Initially Esther is powerless, but eventually she is powerful!* It is all about your relationship with the King. How do you move from "powerless" to "powerful"? *Learn the protocol of the palace!*

THE CROWDS SEEK BREAD FROM HIM

Like the Israelites of the Exodus in the Old Testament who were mirac-ulously fed in a wilderness, large crowds in the New Testament of five thousand and of four thousand men plus their families received miracle bread and meat from Jesus and looked for more. This place of unforeseen blessing was virtually outside of "the courts of God" but within range of His blessing. Many of us who receive compassionate blessings from God often lock Him into a permanent box, a stereotype of "Emergency Need-Supplier" and "Breadgiver."

Often those with no relationship to God (even atheists) cry out to Him in times of need, but quickly revert to type as soon as bread is plentiful, their bellies are filled, or the crisis is over. Even more slip out the door when *cost* is applied to their experience with God because they prefer instead to look for the next free ride or titillating adventure.

This reminds me of historical scenes where a king parades through the streets of old London, Paris, or Persia while thousands of seemingly loyal subjects line the streets for treats or money thrown out to the crowd by the king's servants.

This is an almost irrational and non-relational mindset toward the Great King and His kingdom. Those who yell, shout, and scramble for isolated blessings don't really *know* Him. They see His passing presence as a rare blessing that cannot be counted upon day after day.

While it is true that Esther's becoming the king's choice was a rare and virtually unprecedented event, it is not unprecedented for you and me! Our King of Kings has invited us to *boldly approach His throne.* This is not a spiritual lottery! But there is a protocol of the palace, a way to enter into His presence.

THEY ONLY WANTED HIM TO STAY *IF* . . .

It happened the day Jesus entered Jerusalem on a donkey. The crowd wanted to make Him king, if only for a day. He could remain a popularly acclaimed king only if He would remove Rome's influence and restore Israel to its old glory under David and Solomon.

The crowds hailed Jesus as a miracle worker with a bright future and as a political leader who would change government and right wrongs. A populist leader—with miracle power to boot! Everything was fine with these folks until an untamed God who was larger than their theology popped their political bubble.

These types usually stay outside the gates of relationship, unwilling to learn the protocol of worship—waiting on the randomness of God to pass by their station in life. They seem to never understand that you can attract God's attention through the protocol of worship!

SOME SEE JESUS AS A GREAT TEACHER

Some even honor the law of God and have great respect for those who teach it well with authority. They tend to be more religious than most, possess more than average knowledge of God's Word, and generally *apply it less effectively* than they should. They make a god out of the law and never meet the Author!

Some halt at the threshold of the next level. They feel the tug to move to the next room in the palace, but they don't have the proper stamp on their spiritual passport. They can comprehend that we "enter His gates with thanksgiving," but they stumble at entering "His courts with praise."

They find it difficult to worship when there's nothing apparent for which to be thankful!

This is the place of mixture, where petitions and requests are mixed with praise for God. "Thankful" is a good place to be, but "praise" will take you closer. It is a level of relationship but not the closest of relationships. There is still a strong element of "You scratch my back and I'll scratch Yours" overshadowing some of these activities.

ONE ROOM AWAY ...

Knowing who He is and drawing as close as possible are two different things. All twelve of the disciples *knew* who Jesus was (including Judas, who betrayed Him using the power of recognition and personal knowledge). Of the twelve, there were three who drew as close as possible—Peter, James, and John. These three were called together from their fishing boats, and these three accompanied Him to the Mount of Transfiguration.

In the hour of the King's greatest need in the Garden of Gethsemane, the twelve again aligned themselves in specific levels of intimacy (whether by choice or by divine design, we do not know). Nine stayed behind at one point, and the three again accompanied Him to the place of prayer and agony. Then He moved still farther, until He was a "stone's throw away," and began to pray.

All of this shows that there are those in privileged positions of intimacy who may approach His throne anytime and anywhere. These men and women correspond to the seven "princes of the face," who had ready access to the throne and ear of the king. They hold rank, exercise responsibility, and even function in a part-time "priestly" role on behalf of others. Yet there is still another level in the protocol of His presence.

There are some who love Him simply because He is.

John the beloved was a fisherman, a tough man whose tender love got the best of him. He loved Jesus passionately and came to consistently seek His heart more than His hand.

In the gospel that he penned, John even described himself as "the disciple whom Jesus loved" and as the one who leaned his head on the Master's chest. It is possible that the intimate relationship John had with Jesus produced at times a measure of envy in the others.[25]

Again, another great example of extravagant love was the woman with the alabaster box and the unceasing tears. This woman—and countless other people like her—epitomizes the words of Jesus when He reprimanded the critics of Mary's uninhibited display of love:

> Do you see this woman? I came into your house. You did not give me any water for my feet, but she wet my feet with her tears and wiped them with her hair. You did not give me a kiss, but this woman, from the time I entered, has not stopped kissing my feet. You did not put oil on my head, but she has poured perfume on my feet. Therefore, I tell you, *her many sins have been forgiven— for she loved much. But he who has been forgiven little loves little.*[26]

START AT HIS FEET, WORSHIP TO HIS HEART

When you start from nothing and worship Him who is everything, you start in humility at His feet and worship your way to His heart. Although you ask for nothing, you receive all the abundance of His hands and wisdom in the process. This is "alabaster-box-breaking worship," the kind of worship that God cannot ignore or leave unanswered.[27] This is a perfect picture of how we should "boldly approach the throne." *The protocol of worship will usher an uninvited interloper into a "throne zone" experience.*

The bold love of a forgiven worshiper, Mary Magdalene, positioned her for a unique mission that required her to seek out the disheartened and frightened male disciples. It was to her that the resurrected Christ whispered, "Mary, you go tell the disciples everything is all right."[28]

The Lord has always whispered intimate secrets to box-breaking worshipers! Secrets that disciples will have to figure out for themselves. Do you realize He will tell worshipers things that He won't tell anybody else? He can whisper into their ears because of the intimacy of the moment. The Scripture says, "The Lord confides in those who fear Him."[29] The original language seems to imply that could be intimacy whispered between lovers on a couch.

He loves to manifest His glory and reveal His secrets in rooms filled with the fragrance of our box-breaking worship. In the majesty of those moments, the air is thick with "presence"; it is as if God is so close you could cut the air.

If you ever learn how to act in the palace and how to react in His presence, you will have mastered the protocol that will give you access to the King.

YIELD TO THE PROTOCOL AND LEARN THE WAYS OF THE KING

In every house there is a right way and a wrong way to do things. Yield to the protocol and learn the ways of the King. Esther was schooled in the "palace way." She learned how to walk, how to talk, how to bow just enough, and how to move with regal bearing through a crowded room in a way that won the favor of all who saw her—especially the king.

One day during a moment of leisure, I just happened to be channel-surfing through the myriad of television channels when a program caught my attention. The producers of this show set out to do a makeover for a young woman who dreamed of becoming a model. They began by connecting her with a modeling agent who told her, "Okay, I will make you into a model, but *you must listen to me.*"

The first thing the agent did was to take his young protégée to a top-notch hairstyling salon. The young woman cried when she understood what the stylist proposed to do, and she told him she didn't like it. Things were at an impasse until the agent stepped in to say, "Look, it's up to you: Either you listen to these stylists—they know what they are doing—or you do it your way. *Do you want to be a model or not?*"

Suddenly it dawned on her: *It's not about what I like. These people understand the intense gaze of public scrutiny.* At that point she told them, "Do whatever you want."

Then the agent told her, "I am going to take you to a studio where someone will teach you how to walk." She was offended and said, "I know how to walk." Unmoved, the agent replied, "You don't know *how to walk* where you are about to *have to walk.* You can't just clomp onto the stage." (You can't just clomp your way through the King's court, either!)

They literally put a book on this young woman's head and taught her how to refine her stride so she wouldn't bob up and down or cause the book to fall through sudden or ungraceful movements. She learned exactly how to pivot and turn as if on a fashion runway.

Then the agent worked with her wardrobe and fashion accessories, saying, "Look, you don't look good in that color. You look much better in this color with this combination." They went through the whole process of redesigning her personal makeup techniques, fashion choices, and public demeanor.

One time the wannabe model called home and told her mother, "Mom, I don't know if I can do this. They don't like me. They're trying to make me into somebody else." When she complained to the agent, he said, "You are exactly right. You weren't a model. And we *are* trying to make you into somebody else. Do you want to be yourself, or do you want to be a model?" (Some of us are more intent on "being ourselves" than on being worshipers!)

When it was all said and done, the young woman went on camera and said, "I can't believe it. Now it's natural for me to walk this way. It feels natural for me to act this way." I was awestruck by the vivid contrast between the before-and-after pictures. This was a young lady who now walked with confidence, who now understood the fact that every eye would be on her and every move would be studied. She walked differently, talked differently, and looked differently. She was ready for the public.

My question for you is, "Are you ready for His presence?"

Determine that you want the King, then learn the protocol of His presence and prioritize Him! It is time for the finger of God to carve His initials in the fleshly walls of your heart. You will never forget it. With one crook of the finger—a slight beckoning—you are now an insider! Move inside the palace and next to the King.

If you ever break open your heart and fully follow the protocol of His presence, you will discover for yourself how He turns a peasant into a princess . . . a wannabe into a worshiper!

The experience of Mary, the alabaster-box-breaker, illustrates the transforming miracle in the protocol of His presence:

> And behold, a woman in the city who was a sinner, when she knew that Jesus sat at the table in the Pharisee's house, brought an alabaster flask of fragrant oil, and stood at His feet behind Him weeping; and she began to wash His feet with her tears, and wiped them with the hair of her head; and she kissed His feet and anointed them with the fragrant oil. Now when the Pharisee who had invited Him saw this, he spoke to himself, saying, *"This Man, if He were a prophet, would know who and what manner of woman this is who is touching Him, for she is a sinner."*[30]

When she first walked into the room, they said, "If He knows what kind of person she is, He won't let her get close." Then an incredible transformation began to take place through her worship.

HE CAN ALTER YOUR DESTINY AND CHANGE YOUR REPUTATION

She thought she was washing His feet, but even while she anointed Him, *He was cleansing her reputation and transforming her destiny.* She was never again referred to as "that manner of woman . . . a sinner" in God's Word. She was immortalized by Jesus as one of the ultimate examples of a true worshiper. When you follow the protocol of His presence and worship Him, the King can alter your destiny and change your reputation forever.

> God is no respecter of persons, but He *does* play favorites.

Ask the woman at the well. After only a few minutes with Jesus in Samaria, she was so transformed that though a woman with a ruined reputation, she could now go back and lead her whole village to the truth, even though she couldn't keep five marriages together before her encounter with the Master.[31] What a transformation!

Do you need your destiny altered? Would you like to see your future changed? No matter how unqualified you are, no matter what your past failures keep telling you, your future is bright if you are a worshiper. It is the inevitable conclusion for anyone who discovers and follows the protocol of His presence—*worship.*

The presence of God *can* alter your future if you become a broken-hearted, box-breaking, fragrantly weeping worshiper of the King. He will transform you into a royal heir and a princess—once you learn the purpose for the oil of worship stored in your heart.

His presence is waiting to receive your worship. Break the alabaster box of your heart and pour out the precious oil of your praise and worship. Pour it upon Him!

God is no respecter of persons, but He *does* play favorites. He will do some things for some people that He won't do for others. Those who learn what the King favors can become favorites. Anybody can become a favorite! Anybody can become an Esther! You can stand out from the crowd. The King responds to those who have learned the protocol of His presence. They've mastered the art of how to live as royalty. This protocol of the palace is all predicated upon preparation and worship.

When you draw near to the King in love and worship, He immediately responds to the slightest petitions of your heart. Why? You are not presenting them from the formality of the courtroom. You are not shouting them from the gatehouses.

Move past the gates of thanksgiving! Pass through the courts of praise! Enter the place of intimacy reserved for true worshipers. Go through the veil and enter the Holy of Holies, where His presence is found. Intimacy preempts intruders!

Worship is how you handle yourself in the presence of the King.

> Worship is how you handle yourself in the presence of the King.

CHAPTER 4

INTIMACY AND INFLUENCE

How Relationship Trumps Protocol

Perhaps you have heard the old saying "It's not *what* you know, it's *who* you know." These words are not buried somewhere in a forgotten section of the Bible, but the truth contained in this cliché is demonstrated in the Bible from the front to the back. The influence of intimate friends and family shows up in the everyday events of your own life.

From time to time I am privileged to take my children with me during my travels. It is more difficult now that they are older with busy schedules of their own, but I still insist on their accompanying me on occasion.

No matter who I may be talking to, there are certain things—or certain *faces*—that are guaranteed to attract my attention and reshuffle my priorities. Very often I meet with dignitaries as part of my duties. However, if during one of those meetings I see the irresistible face of one of my daughters peeping through a window or a slightly cracked door, I get distracted. I know that perhaps I shouldn't, but I can't help myself—I am a doting daddy!

You may be able to guess what happens next. I will say, "Would you excuse me for a moment? Uh, ladies and gentlemen, someone, er, something important has come up that I must tend to. I'll be right back."

What would cause me to interrupt an important meeting? The appearance of the face of someone I love and the immense value I place on that person diverts me from lesser matters. The father in me stands up and pushes one priority above all others.

This doesn't happen simply because someone submits petitions to me on the basis of some formal obligation. I do not change my schedule, interrupt conversations, or suspend meetings simply because someone with a title presents a very good idea. Yet by merely presenting her face and flashing her smile, my daughter presents a powerful petition for my attention from the *intimacy of relationship*. (Of course, I've taught my daughters not to interrupt needlessly or to misuse their privileges of access—*not that they always heed that admonition.*)

I don't mean to make light of the power of God's countless promises in His Word to us as believers. I live by them, stand upon them, and chart my course according to them. In fact, you can reference all the legal codes and intercessory petitions you want to, intending to use them to approach God in a demanding posture. But there may be a better way!

With finger pointed at chapter and verse, you may judicially say, "Now, Lord, You promised *this*! And Your Word says *that*." Yes, you can do things this way because God *did* make us promises, and He always *does* keep His given Word. It is also true that we read in the Bible there are times and places to offer petitions, prayers, and requests to Him—*and some times may be better than others.*[1]

> PROTOCOL *of the* PALACE
> 5. Influence flows from intimacy, and access comes from relationship.

Esther teaches us that *influence flows from intimacy, and access comes from relationship.* We can be secure in the knowledge that He won't forget what He promised; His promises are rooted in His *love* for us. I read somewhere that "God so *loved* . . . that He *gave*. . . ."[2] First He loved; then He gave.

Have you ever taken your children with you as you tended to errands around town? Perhaps you promised them a treat if their behavior warranted it. Did you notice that they felt it necessary to remind you at every stop about their potential treat? It is usually phrased "Dad—you promised" or "Daddy, don't forget my ice cream."

While it is entirely possible that *I* might forget, our heavenly Father *cannot* forget! If He promised, just stay close to Him and He will reward!

Constant nagging about His promise *could* be unbelief in a different cloak. There is a better way to secure your reward. Right relationship and staying close to Dad all day guarantees your moment of favor!

This is the *better way*—the way of intimacy and relationship. This precedent of revealing something good and holy and then following with something even better and higher *has happened before.*

Paul the apostle discusses the virtues and benefits of all of the powerful spiritual gifts in 1 Corinthians 12, yet he ends the chapter with these words: "Earnestly desire the *best* gifts. And yet *I show you a more excellent way.*"[3] Then he launches his unforgettable "love chapter," extolling the unmatched power of God's love revealed in our everyday lives. Love is a better way. *Intimacy with Christ is more powerful than petitions legally presented.*

What could be better than formally reminding God of His promises and claiming the benefits of those promises according to His Word? I agree that formal petitions based on God's rock-solid promises are good and right, but we are told that God knows about all of our needs even before we ask Him.[4] The truth is that you hardly have to whisper, "Abba . . . Daddy"[5] before He responds in tender love:

"What do you want, son? What can I do for you, My bride?"

When I am approached by sales representatives, employees, or government officials asking for a sale, a raise, or some other document or payment, I am likely to require some clear justification for their request. "Now, you need to prove your point to me. Show me where the benefit is. Tell my why I need to do this, because I'm not convinced yet."

Something totally different happens when my wife or one of my daughters comes in with a request or desire. They don't have to prove something to me, because we have an intimate relationship.

Yes, you can point at God and say, "God, now I want You to do this because You said in chapter 5 and verse 7 that You would do it." Or you can move *beyond* the formal petitions of the court. This is where all of the clothing and trappings of the judge's bench and the legal counselors are exchanged for the relaxed atmosphere reserved for the intimacy of the private family living quarters.

FAMILY MEMBERS BARELY HAVE TO ASK FOR ANYTHING

In the privacy and relaxed intimacy of the family residence, members barely have to ask for anything. They have access to virtually everything. The father of the house simply asks, "Now, what can I do for you?"

When you seek *His face,* your heavenly Father sees *your face* and interrupts the business of heaven to bend down and inquire about your needs!

Esther could never have accomplished what she did in saving the Jewish people from annihilation if she didn't occupy a place of high affection and privilege in the heart of the king.

Esther had a "dry run" early in her married relationship with King Xerxes when her older cousin and adoptive parent, Mordecai, accidentally overheard an assassination plot unfolding.

> One day as Mordecai was on duty at the palace, two of the king's eunuchs, Bigthana and Teresh—who were guards at the door of the king's private quarters—became angry at King Xerxes and plotted to assassinate him. But Mordecai heard about the plot and *passed the information on to Queen Esther.* She then *told the king about it* and *gave Mordecai credit* for the report. When an investigation was made and Mordecai's story was found to be true, the two men were hanged on a gallows. This was all duly recorded in *The Book of the History of King Xerxes' Reign.*[6]

World history would read very differently today had God not planted His young deliverer in the life of Persia's King Xerxes. God moved an unknown Jewish orphan maiden into a pagan harem and orchestrated the unthinkable when she was chosen by Xerxes as his new queen.

As queen of Persia, Esther had *access* to the ear of the king in the royal bedchambers. Remember: *Influence flows from intimacy, and access comes from relationship.*

OLD FRIENDS DREAD THE ARRIVAL OF "THE GIRL OF HIS DREAMS"

How does this work in everyday life? Consider how many times you have seen this particular scenario take place: A young man with a large circle of acquaintances and a smaller circle of close friends suddenly meets "the girl of his dreams."

He may have been acquainted with or even dated five, ten, or a hundred different females in his life, but this time something gripped his heart and wouldn't let go.

Within a matter of days there is grumbling in the camp because suddenly this good friend isn't spending time with his old circle the way he used to. His closest friends may have the hardest time, because someone else is consuming his hours and influencing his choices.

Before he can make a commitment to "go bowling with the guys," he now wants to check with *that girl.* What happened? When this young man developed a relationship with the young lady, she gained privileged access to his heart and his thinking processes.

As their love and commitment to each other becomes more and more intimate (I am *not* speaking of physical intimacy in this example), this young lady's *influence* over his priorities and choices increases.

This is the inevitable way of life, and it is also the inevitable way we should grow in our relationship with God. I am not saying that one person will wrestle away God's attention from others. God is God. He is well able to attend to *all of us* simultaneously, and that is His desire. I am saying that *with relationship comes access, and with intimacy comes influence.*

Moses, the man God chose to deliver the children of Israel from Pharaoh, was successful because of his *relationship* with God, not because of his natural gifts, his abilities, or even his knowledge of the *ways* of God.

He wasn't content to study the "ways" of this fresh manifestation of the God of his ancestors—Moses chose to *walk with God in intimacy* into the unknown, and God blessed him with *even more intimacy.*

With every increase of his intimacy with God, Moses also received an increased ability to *influence* the affairs of men and nations—and even the heart of the Lord. When God declared He would destroy the children of Israel for their unbelief, Moses interceded on their behalf and literally *persuaded Him* to show mercy. There still were consequences for their actions, but God spared the nation.[7]

With relationship comes access, and with intimacy comes influence. Moses' intimate times with God produced the Ten Commandments—the Law—and the prophetic direction to feed and lead more than one million people through a barren wilderness for forty years.

Moses constantly communed with God in the Tent of Meeting (*relationship is cultured, not automatic*), and his relationship created *access.* He spent extended stays with God on Mount Sinai, and when Moses finally returned from those divine appointments, his face reflected the brilliant but fading glory of the residue of God's presence. Even *that* was too much for the children of Israel.[8]

Moses became accustomed to the reflected glory accumulated around the residence of God, but he became dissatisfied with the afterglow of glory. He longed for *more*. When God offered him blessings and power, Moses cried out, "Show me Your glory! Let me see Your face!"[9] (His request was finally granted *after he died*—when he communed with Jesus face to face on the Mount of Transfiguration!)[10]

GOD IS UNIMPRESSED WITH HUMANITY'S BEST

God is unimpressed by even the greatest of human accomplishments, and who can hope to win against God in a battle of wills, domination, conquest, or wealth? Why even mention personal ability? To put things another way, the only way to gain access to *the things of God's kingdom* is through *relationship with the King*.

Again, *with relationship comes access, and with intimacy comes influence.* Even the King of Kings, Jesus Christ, gained *access* to heavenly counsel, strength, and direction during His earthly ministry through old-fashioned *relationship* in prayer to His Father.

EVERYTHING JESUS DID, SAID, AND TAUGHT CAME FROM THE FATHER

Again and again in the Gospels we see Jesus moving away from the crowds to pray alone and commune with the Father. He made it plain that everything He did, said, and taught He received from the Father. His ministry was born and fueled by the intimate relationship they enjoyed.[11]

In *God's Eye View*, I shared this nugget from my treasure trove of father-daughter encounters:

> My girls know that if I made an agreement with them, then I
> will be happy to give them whatever we agreed upon for their

allowance. Yet my girls have learned "a more excellent way." They don't ask for an allowance; *they just ask to take Daddy shopping.*[12]

One time this happened during a conference, and my daughter's request was delivered in the presence of several of my ministry friends. One of the men couldn't help but ask this particular daughter a question, hoping to divert her to another solution for her shopping needs. He said, "You don't want to go shopping with your dad, do you? Why don't you wait and go shopping with your mom?"

She bluntly told him, "No. I'd rather go shopping with my dad." And my friend fell right into the trap when he tried a second attempt at subtle persuasion.

> That was when she delivered the quintessential nugget of wisdom mined by all three of my thoroughly modern daughters: "No, when I go shopping with my mom, I have to beg or talk her into everything. When I go shopping with Dad, *if I just look at it, I get it.*" (I won't bother to describe the look that pastor gave me at that point—he hasn't been on the receiving end of three Tenney girls sashaying into the kitchen over the last two decades.)[13]

Esther was learning this same lesson. Bible scholars and theologians all seem to agree that the book of Esther is a book of God's providence. He is moving to care for His people long before they realize they need His help.

If it is true that *with relationship comes access, and with intimacy comes influence,* then the Jews were in serious trouble the moment Haman showed up in Persia. This foreigner had managed to snag the number two spot in the entire kingdom, and it was apparent that he was dead set against the Jews. As refugees with limited status, the Jews seemed powerless to protect themselves.

The only human being on the planet with the power to save the Jews at that time was the king. Although there is clear indication that King Xerxes' father had passed down his positive attitude toward the Jews to his son early in his life, the book of Esther indicates that he was well on his way to being won over by Haman's anti-Semitic ways.[14]

Ethnic cleansing seems to be the latest rising storm on the horizon of human affairs today, just as it was during Esther's time. It *appeared* as though no one with access—no one intimately connected—to the king even cared about the prognosis for the Jewish people. The future looked grim for those who seemingly had no friends in high places!

GOD PLANTED HIS UNLIKELY "SAVIOR" RIGHT UNDER THE KING'S NOSE

God foresaw all of this in advance. Remember: *With relationship comes access, and with intimacy comes influence.* It was time for God to step in and plant His unlikely but appointed "savior" right under the nose of the king and of the Jews' archenemy. Esther enters the picture.

According to the unchangeable law of the Medes and Persians, there was no hope for the Jewish residents of the Persian empire. It didn't matter where they lived—from Jerusalem to Ethiopia or India, and from Babylon to Susa, death would find them out.

Haman hated the Jews, and he had access to the face of the king through political relationship. He was a master at making formal petitions based on law, rights, and precedents from his privileged position in the king's court.

Satan is the accuser of the brethren. His misplaced sense of justice says, "I *saw* them do it—they are guilty. Wipe them out!"

Lucifer knows the law! But I know the Lawyer. No one has higher access to, or intimacy with, the Father than my Lawyer, my Advocate—Jesus Christ, the Righteous One.

It *really is* who you know! He stands in the court of heaven and refutes the charges, contending that the penalty has been paid!

Haman's problem was similar in that he forgot one all-important fact about life in the king's court: *Whispered words from the place of intimacy can be more powerful than shouted petitions from the court. In fact, words whispered from the pillow of royal intimacy can literally rearrange the future.*

God intervened to make a way where there was no way. He carefully prepared Esther from birth to enter the king's world "through the back door" of the king's house, and He anointed her to win the king's favor and through intimacy to gain *access to his heart.* This gave Esther more influence than Haman could ever hope to enjoy. Do you know that you can have access to the King's heart?

> Whispered words from the place of intimacy can be more powerful than shouted petitions from the court.

> Worship your way to a place of intimacy. One well-placed whisper could change your life!

Remember: *With relationship comes access, and with intimacy comes influence.* This is never truer than in the kingdom of God, where our intimate relationship with Him through worship gives us access to His throne and influence in the world.

Your worship can create your moment—your chance to change destiny!

Prioritize His presence—work on your relationship with the King. Never forget that when you seek *His* face, He remembers *your* face! Relationship has a reward—*Access*!

Your influence with people is often in direct proportion to *the level of intimacy* you have with them! Don't indulge yourself in justifying your "distant personality." The last person you want to call long-distance is God! Worship your way to a place of intimacy. One well-placed whisper could change your life—it could even save a nation!

CHAPTER 5

COURTING A KING

*What Do You Give a Man
Who Has Everything?*

I magine the scene when a young peasant girl[1] named Hadassah looked up to see a richly dressed dignitary from the king's palace coming down the street with armed guards in tow. He had been working his way down a list of names and addresses. Now as agent for the throne he was on his way to the house of Mordecai to "pick up another of the king's maidens."

Like a housewife in the marketplace selecting only the most beautiful fruits, this dignitary was carrying a shopping list pared down to only the most beautiful virgins.

Esther had caught the vigilant eye of the palace scouts. They demanded of her an address and told her to be expecting an escort to the palace within a few days. Flight was futile; they *would* find her, and her beloved Mordecai would suffer the consequences as well if she fled.

The days spent waiting were also spent learning. Mordecai schooled her in as much palace protocol as possible.

She knew the time had come. Weeks of officials researching rumors and interviewing maidens had come to an end. Now the "lucky ones" were being escorted to the palace.

There was nothing left to do but obey the king's decree and appear. The Bible simply says she "was taken."[2] I doubt she fought or even resisted, because it would have been useless and even dangerous. Mordecai told Hadassah *not* to reveal her Jewish heritage, so she had to be careful not to draw undue attention to herself.[3]

Where and how she gained the "public" name of Esther is unknown. Perhaps it was in the same manner that the names of Daniel, Hananiah, Mishael, and Azariah were changed without resistance to Belteshazzar, Shadrach, Meshach, and Abed-Nego. Hadassah became Esther.[4]

Agents of the king had spread out into all 127 provinces of the king's realm. Everyone surmised that King Xerxes' envoys would have a difficult time finding an equal to Queen Vashti's beauty. No one mused even for a second that they could find someone who exceeded her astonishing good looks.

However, none of the agents really expected to find a polished regal replacement for Queen Vashti waiting for them, prepared and ready for marriage to the king. They weren't looking for perfection. They were looking for *potential*!

As the beauty pageant net stretched across twenty-three nations and countless cultures within those nations, the king's men reaped a harvest of the most promising girls dwelling within the shadow of the Medo-Persian empire. (Perhaps some enterprising princes or scheming fathers politically inserted their daughters into the process.)

When these young virgins were brought in from the outlying countryside to prepare for their "blind date" with the king, only a handful of them would have ever even seen the mighty Xerxes. Those few may have lived in Susa, where they would have seen him in a royal procession parading through the city en route to a royal hunting trip or after a military victory.

We know this much with virtual certainty—the king was also on a blind date with destiny. He didn't know what any of these women looked like, but *he was searching for a new queen.*

ESTHER KNEW THE INEVITABLE WAS UPON HER

Esther and her guardian, Mordecai, knew the inevitable was upon them. When the king's agents came for her and others in her area, I don't think they dragged her kicking and screaming into the palace. The Esther we will come to know probably thought, *I have to go, so I will go.*

When Esther was taken with the other virgins, I believe that she (1) simply submitted herself to her destiny; and (2) *did not realize* she was taking that step of divine destiny through the orchestration of God (that became clear only *later* in her life).

In the aftermath of her selection and at the time of the "beauty pageant," Esther had to prepare herself in an unusual way. It was necessary to remove every sign of her Jewish heritage from her outward appearance, speech, and mannerisms. This might have been more difficult than one would imagine.

In many international cities you find street hawkers or low-level con men whose main purpose is to separate unwitting tourists from their money. These people have the unique skill of accurately calling out your nationality as they make their sales pitch: "Hey, American. Do you want. . . ?" Amazingly, they can often determine from the kind of shoes on your feet whether you are, for instance, Canadian, Spanish, or German. Cultural connections are not that easily concealed.

Under normal circumstances, it would have been easy for Persians of any rank or station to identify Esther as Jewish by her language, dress, and mannerisms. Perhaps even her jewelry would have given away her Jewish identity.

That the great Persian pageant took place in Susa, the summer capital at the time, meant that everything Persian would be considered normal; anything else would not. Esther's first task was to shed everything that would identify her as a Jewish maiden, a significant challenge for a girl raised in an ancient Jewish home. She could not even afford for the sandals on her feet, much less the garment on her body, to give away her ethnic origin.

Esther had no concept of how to court a king, but God did. This age-old tradition of winning the heart of the beloved is vastly different from the freewheeling and haphazard method we moderns call "dating."

In courtship, the goal is to win a pledge of marriage by building rela-tionship; the ultimate aim is permanent union through commitment. In relatively recent times, courtship has been supplanted by dating, the prac-tice of "going out to try out" numerous suitors. The hope is that you some-how "find the match that fits the best." The popular emphasis within dating is usually placed on fleeting moments of romantic high points rather than on developing in-depth, caring relationships between individuals.

You "court" someone under mutually understood boundaries or guide-lines of protocol. The two parties spend time together in preplanned social activities—usually in one of the family homes. These events are often mon-itored or administered by outside parties such as parents, chaperones, or—as in Esther's case—*the king's chamberlains.*

As I've said, I'm convinced that God orchestrated Esther's initial preparation from her birth through her childhood. The Bible says Esther was "lovely and beautiful."[5] The Hebrew term translated *lovely* refers to her outward beauty, and the term for *beautiful* seems to mean literally that Esther was "good through and through,"[6] describing her internal beauty.

ONE YEAR FOR ONE NIGHT

Again, as lovely and as beautiful as Esther was, she still wasn't good enough. As incredible as it seems, her final preparation for one night with the king took twelve months of intensive training. *One year preparing for one night.*

It would have been foolish for the king's officials to take someone off the farm and stick her in front of Xerxes and have her awkwardly stammer, "Yo, King!" Especially when she still had dirt under her fingernails or the smell of earth on her clothing.

Every bridal candidate submitted to extensive preparation to remove every odor, habit, blemish, or spot that would be out of place before the throne of the great ruler.

Esther was washed, scrubbed, and immersed in special cleansing herbs and spices. She was given free rein to dress in any nice garment she chose, and she was taught how to walk and carry herself like royalty.

Spending twelve months with spices doesn't mean they only took oil baths. They were also *scrubbed* with them.[7] This was *some* ancient exfoliation process! Can you imagine how sweet she smelled? Just how soft was her skin?

As part of my ministry duties, I often travel in various parts of the world. Some of the cultures in which I spend a great deal of time seem to have a particular penchant for garlic. This spice is known to possess powerful health benefits, but it also packs a pungent odor! I've noticed that even when people in these cultures have sweet *breath,* the smell of garlic seems to ooze out of their *pores*! Perhaps the process Esther endured included internal as well as external cleansing—an ancient Persian form of what we call a detox program today. This much we do know: their diet *was* changed.

Remember, young Esther was soaked in the oil baths of bitter and sweet spices to transform the very fragrance of her body. Bear in mind this was the *king's* oil—an exclusive fragrance. You soak in the king's oil to smell like the king.

When we soak in *His* oils of repentance and full surrender, accompanied with thanksgiving, praise, and worship, *then* we exchange our earthly stench for heavenly fragrance. We can actually begin to smell like heaven. The Scripture says (of the disciples), they "took note" of them that they had been with Jesus. I wonder if we could also say that they "took note" of them that they smelled like Jesus?

Ironically, this picture is echoed in a royal decree issued by Xerxes' father, King Darius, authorizing support to the Levite priests restoring temple worship in Jerusalem and encouraging them in a nearly prophetic proclamation:

> That which they have need of, both young bullocks, and rams, and lambs, for the burnt offerings of the God of heaven, wheat, salt, wine, and oil, according to the appointment of the priests which are at Jerusalem, let it be given them day by day without fail: That they may offer *sacrifices of sweet savours unto the God of heaven,* and pray for the life of the king, and of his sons.[8]

Esther submitted herself to the protocol of palace preparation for one reason: *The only way to be transformed and conformed into an acceptable bride for the king was to submit to the protocols of the palace—including soaking in the oil!*

We in the body of Christ experience transformation when the anointing of God descends upon us. Understood like this, I would have to say the anointing is for Him—not us![9] The oil is *on* us, but it is *for* Him!

The king provided oil and spices to the maidens to transform them from earthy-smelling peasants to divinely aromatic princesses. Remember: When the Lord pours His fragrant anointing oil over you, it is so that He, in His holiness, can stand to be in the same room! That is when you begin to smell less earthy and more heavenly.

LOST IN THE FRAGRANCE
OF THE MOMENT

Our problem is that we often get so taken up and lost in the fragrance of the moment that we totally forget the purpose behind it. It is as if we dance up to the veil, the dividing line between the earthly and the heavenly, but we never actually enter into the presence of God. As I noted in *The God Chasers*:

> The King's chamber, the Holy of Holies, awaits the anointed. The holy anointing oil was literally rubbed on and into everything in the Holy Place, *including the garments of the priest.* They then took "powdered perfume" to anoint the very atmosphere.
>
> *And he* [Aaron and his successors] *shall take a censer full of burning coals of fire from off the altar before the* LORD, *and his hands full of sweet incense beaten small, and bring it within the veil:*
>
> *And he shall put the incense upon the fire before the* LORD, *that the cloud of the incense may cover the mercy seat that is upon the testimony, that he die not.* (Leviticus 16:12–13 KJV)

Under the ordinances of the Old Testament, the last thing the high priest did before he entered into the Holy of Holies was to place a handful of incense (symbolic of the anointing) into a censer and thrust his hands and the censer through the veil to make a dense screen of smoke. Why? To "cover the mercy seat . . . that he die not" (Leviticus 16:13b). The priest had to make enough smoke to camouflage or conceal his flesh from God's presence.[10]

> Sometimes the King makes you wait just to purify the outcome.

In an era of instant gratification, patience with the process of God is a rare commodity. The fact that these maidens were kept waiting for twelve months probably frustrates much of our modern theology. Perhaps this also broadens our understanding of the term "lady-in-waiting"!

The twelve-month waiting period also did something else. If any of the girls happened to be pregnant, it would show up—literally! This time period insured that anything birthed would be of the king. *Sometimes the King makes you wait just to purify the outcome.*

"WHAT ARE YOU *DOING*, PASTOR?"

Remember, Esther spent a full year preparing for one night with the king. We get upset if we don't have "revival" after a week of fasting or a series of special worship services. Church leaders often pay a dear price if they persevere to lead special worship services every Friday or Saturday night for six years. Critics batter them with the question, "What are you *doing?*"

It is hard to quantify genuine hunger and a burning desire for more of God. It usually causes individual believers and entire congregations to act and worship more like blind Bartimaeus, desperately crying out to Jesus from a dusty ditch in Jericho, rather than like the proud-praying Pharisee's pontificating on the steps of the temple. One found favor by "brailling" for Jesus—the others missed Him with eyes wide open!

Attempts to set these actions of the heart into concrete formulas or revival rules nearly always become empty religious rituals! This often doesn't have anything to do with the worship offered *in spirit and in truth* that God seeks.[11]

We should applaud and encourage any church congregation willing to seek God's face in repentance, praise, and worship in fifty-two extra services per year for six years, or even six months. (I wouldn't be surprised to learn that God is delighted to see fifty-two extra *minutes* of uninhibited worship in many of His churches.)

WHAT DOES HUNGER OR THIRST HAVE TO DO WITH GOD?

Preparatory, soaking worship like this is hard to transcribe into a set program. *Passion cannot be programmed.* Even these words aren't a formula or a recommendation, because revival can't be "produced" by any equation. This is all about demonstrating genuine hunger and thirst for God and His kingdom. What do hunger or thirst have to do with God and the church? Ask King David.

> As the deer pants for the water brooks, so pants my soul for You, O God. My soul thirsts for God, for the living God.[12]

A satiated soul sips; a desperate soul gulps! "Panting" probably wouldn't fit too well in many modern church programs!

Don't hurry the process!

Drink deeply and long. . . .

Whether we talk about Esther in the past or the people of God in the present, we don't just leap from a place of peasantry into the position of princess. If it took Esther one year to prepare for that one night with the king of Persia, how should the church prepare for her encounter with the King of Kings? We must *never* underestimate the potential of one night.

> If you would become a queen, you must first court the King.

Remember: It only takes one night to change your destiny. Just one encounter with God can alter your future! Mere seconds in the manifest presence of God turned a murderer named Saul into a martyr named Paul. One encounter with God can change your life forever! It doesn't take long, but you *do* have to prepare if you want to be ready when it happens. Never underestimate the potential for one night, but *also never underestimate the preparation necessary for that night*!

Esther prepared so that she would be ready. She worked hard to master the art of becoming a princess. If you would "court" a king, you must learn to act like a princess. That includes learning how to *walk as a princess.*

The floors and surfaces of the King's courts are smooth and made of polished and precious materials, unlike the dusty streets and rocky byways outside. Care must be taken that one doesn't "slip up" in the palace. Proud steps and arrogance like hobnail boots echo harshly and are frowned upon there . . . everyone must walk softly and humbly before the King of Kings.

Stomping boots may be necessary in the warlike atmosphere outside the palace. Inside the palace, soft slippers, prayerful posture, and a humble approach are necessary. All paths lead to Him through the Cross. Some go directly, others move closer slowly and in roundabout ways, but *all* of them must follow the protocol of His presence. God is holy, but we are not, unless *He* makes us holy.

Just as Esther was prepared and transformed to act and smell like a princess, God has also called the church to be His bride. *If you would become a queen, you must first court the King.*

Courting the King means placing priority on His needs, not yours. In a society filled with a "me" mindset, this is a simple but rare commodity. The King says it's all about Him—*and it is*! God has this incredible idea that church is about Him!

REPULSIVE *IN COMPARISON TO* THE FRAGRANCE AROUND THE KING

It is unlikely that Esther came from a rural area, and perhaps she didn't reek of barnyard smells. She may have even had the most pleasant aromatic signature in her neighborhood, but *in comparison to the fragrances around the king and his chambers,* even her best scent may have been repulsive to those accustomed to the royal court.

Can you imagine some beauty contestant shuffling into the opulent presence of the king of Persia wearing her finest village clothes but still reeking with the common fragrance of a lower realm? When a true princess enters the room, everyone around her should notice something new in the air—a *sweet* and inviting fragrance. It is a fragrance reserved for the king, and the king alone. In the kingdom of God, this fragrance of great value is praise and worship offered to Him from the heart in spirit and in truth.

When people of different cultures travel internationally, they may notice that some of the houses they visit have peculiar smells to them. It isn't because the people who live there are especially dirty. It has to do with the foods they eat and the lifestyles they follow.

If someone from the Farm Belt visits friends in the commercial fishing industry along the Atlantic Seaboard or in the Pacific Northwest, they may wonder if they will ever escape the smell of fish.

Folks from the coasts may also have some interesting comments about the pig farms, cattle and sheep ranches, dairy barns, and chicken houses they encounter in Middle America.

While these smells may be perfectly acceptable in their area or in the context of everyday work environments, they are frowned upon in exclusive atmospheres.

I had a pastor-friend whose passion was fishing. Once, while enjoying a well-deserved day on the water, he suddenly remembered an afternoon wedding that he was supposed to officiate. Racing for the shore, then driving maniacally to the church, he arrived just in time to wash his hands and put on an emergency suit he always left at the office.

Outwardly he appeared to be okay. He breathed a sigh of relief, only to have his wife tell him as he walked onto the wedding stage that he "smelled fishy"! Humiliated, he tried to spritz himself with cologne to mask the odor. What he *really* needed was a good soaking!

Spend time soaking in the anointed atmosphere of worship. If you intend to win the heart of the King, some changes will be necessary. *Wait* upon the Lord and learn how to court the King. Our earthy fragrance may not be offensive to our fellow inhabitants—but *they* are not who we are after!

God ordained that the bride of the Lamb smell like a princess, but she was also expected to talk as a princess. The King gives you a new song and a new way of thinking to frame a new language of faith, hope, and joy in a new realm.

Esther had to learn a new way to address those around her. She was taught how to talk like a queen instead of a peasant. To be welcome in the palace you must learn how to "walk the walk and talk the talk." Royalty must even learn a new way to address enemies, using all of the authority they have been given. Where once Esther might have cowered before her enemies, or at least have lowered her eyes or moved aside, now she must look into their eyes as a ruler, a privileged member of the royal court, and an intimate of the king.

I am not speaking of religious jargon and tired clichés. *The practiced persona of self-righteousness may impress others, but it will offend the King.*

EVERY ROUGH PLACE WAS SMOOTHED OFF, EVERY BLEMISH REMOVED

You already know that Esther spent an *entire year* bathing each night in fragrant oils and sweet spice baths, but the chamberlain also required her to undergo special body treatments as preparation for her impending encounter with the king.

Every rough place was smoothed off, every blemish removed; and, in accordance with Persian tradition, it is likely that all body hair was removed as well. She even *ate* certain spices such as myrrh as part of the preparation protocol.

Esther looked good, and can you imagine what she smelled like after soaking in those fragrant oils for a year? The fragrances probably exuded from every pore of her skin, from her hair, and even from her clothing. You could probably smell her long before you ever saw her approach!

No matter where she went in the royal compound, I imagine that any young man who managed to come near her in some way would be riveted by her beauty and drawn by her sweet fragrance.

Historically, it's likely she was strictly separated from all males except the king's eunuchs. *What if* one of the more impetuous young members of the king's court came close and dared to make a pass?

"Hey, Esther. You smell good. Come here, let's talk."

"Sorry, I can't talk to you right now."

"Yeah, but we need to talk."

"No, I can't."

"But you smell good."

"It's not your oil and it's not your fragrance. I may smell good to you, but the fragrant oil comes *from* the king and it's *for* the king."

JUST REMEMBER THE *REAL PURPOSE* OF THE ANOINTING

When we lay aside our private religious agendas long enough to worship God, many of us discover we have taken on a new fragrance—we have been anointed by His Spirit. The King's oil of anointing makes you preach better, it makes you teach better, it makes you sing better. The power of His anointing is so strong that it even makes you look better and smell better to other people.

Just remember that the *real purpose* of the anointing process is to prepare you for God's presence and to turn a peasant into a princess.

What if I walked up to a lady sitting in the front row at a meeting, extended my hand toward her, and said:

> Don't flirt with lower lovers — save yourself for the King.

"Hello, can you smell that?"

"Yes, it is very nice. I like it."

"That is my cologne. I didn't put it on for you—I put it on for my wife. I may happen to smell nice to you, but it is the *by-product* of my effort to smell nice for my bride."

Sometimes, if we're not careful, our wonderful church meetings may turn into a spiritual cologne-smelling party or just another department-store praise bar. We marvel and revel in the anointing of the singer, of the choir, or of the preacher. We can easily forget that the whole purpose of the anointing is to prepare us for the King's presence.

God is tired of seeing us prostitute His anointing for our own purposes. Remember that the King's oil is for the King's presence. We must stop prostituting the anointing.

The anointing is not to make us sound good, look good, or smell good to man. That happens as a by-product, but the real purpose of the anointing is to give us favor in the King's chamber.

Our flesh stinks to God and the anointing makes us acceptable to the King. It's God's process of turning peasants into princesses—prospective brides-to-be![13]

CAMOUFLAGE THE STENCH

We should be thankful that God anoints us to sing, to testify, to serve as deacons, or to preach. But remember that the real purpose of the anointing is to camouflage the stench of human flesh so that the King can stand to be in our presence and so that we may be allowed to be in His.[14]

This is not about courting the favor of flesh or attempting solely to gain man's approval. This is about courting the King and *finding favor with the King*!

Don't flirt with lower lovers—save yourself for the King.

"Esther, why don't you talk to any of those other young men?"
"Because I don't have time for lower lovers—I'm saving myself for the King!"

THE ANOINTING CHANGES EVERYTHING ABOUT YOU

The by-product of being prepared for the King's presence is that many of the people around you may also be attracted to and appreciate the fragrance of your life. Many will approve of you when you are preparing for the King. It changes you and transforms your personality. The anointing alters everything about you.

Esther *prepared* for her encounter with the King. She got ready, she soaked, she learned how to walk, she learned how to talk, and she dressed for success. This was of ultimate importance. *The King was tired of girlfriends.* He was going to choose one candidate to be queen.

God is also tired of girlfriends, those who just want to date Him for the candy and the gifts. The King of Kings is looking for a bride. A bride is someone who is more interested in the giver than the gifts! That is spelled *c-o-m-m-i-t-m-e-n-t.*

It is not my intention to earn an "X" rating for this book, but the truth is that the culture of the time permitted the king of Persia to pick any woman he wanted. It was understood in that pagan culture that just because the king slept with a woman didn't mean he had to marry her (the kings of Israel and Judah also had primary wives and secondary wives— even though this clearly was not God's preference). With that in mind, clearly something more attracted Xerxes to Esther. It was not some misplaced sense of obligation.

Some way, somehow, all of the careful preparations paid off when Esther was chosen to be more than a girlfriend. The king got *serious* with her.

Do you realize the King of Kings wants to get serious with you? He wants to take your relationship to the next level! The King is talking commitment! (And when the King talks commitment, He means forever!) How committed are you?

Are you intent on wooing and winning the heart of the King?

What do you give someone who already has everything? How do you win his heart?

How do you court a King? He seemingly lacks nothing. Your trivial offerings could even be construed as an insult.

How do you gain favor?

You must understand that the King has a "weakness."

> But after Xerxes' anger had cooled, *he began thinking about Vashti.*[15]

The King wants a bride. You are His only need; His only weakness is your worship!

What do you give someone who has everything?

Yourself.

CHAPTER 6

THE SECRET OF THE CHAMBERLAIN

Finding Favor With the King

The day Esther was crowned Queen of Persia, a chorus of at least 399 beautiful women from twenty-three nations wondered, *What is Esther's secret? Why was she chosen? Why not me?*

The most disappointed members of the group, I suspect, were the Persian noblewomen who learned that even their bloodline and family lineage couldn't overpower Esther's secret attraction. None of them understood why Persia's powerful king chose an unknown foreigner as queen, even rejecting the daughters of Persia's blue-blood nobility.

People in the church today ask similar questions for similar reasons. Their concern isn't so much about "who will be queen?" but "who does God love the most?" They wonder, *Why do the prayers of certain people seem to be answered more than the prayers of others? Is there some secret formula or personal asset that somehow puts them closer to God?*

GOD IS NO RESPECTER OF PERSONS

The apostle Peter declared that God is no "respecter of persons" or of human rank.[1] The Creator loves us all, and the one measure of God's love for each of us is the immeasurable worth of His own Son's life. Even so, there *are* certain things that foster intimacy with divinity. Again: *God is no respecter of persons, but He does play favorites!*

Esther is about to demonstrate to us an important life lesson: *Listen to the King's chamberlain.* King Xerxes had given his chamberlain, Hegai, complete charge over the house of women.

> Now when the turn of Esther, the daughter of Abihail the uncle of Mordecai, who had taken her for his daughter, was come to go in unto the king, *she required nothing but what Hegai the king's chamberlain, the keeper of the women, appointed.* And Esther

obtained *favour* in the sight of *all* them that looked upon her.[2]

It is obvious that Hegai was no ordinary eunuch. Hundreds of eunuchs served in the king's palace and official courts, but Hegai was an officer of the state, a highly placed *chamberlain* assigned to be "keeper of the women."[3]

Various translations of Scripture use differing terms to describe the position of Hegai. A combination of two terms used most often seem to best describe his role: Hegai was a *eunuch* and a *chamberlain*. In terms of a Persian palace, it was understood that anyone who was a chamberlain (especially if their area of responsibility was to care for women in the harem or the royal quarters) was also a eunuch.

> Listen to the King's chamberlain.

A eunuch was a man who had been cruelly castrated so that the king would be able to trust his motives. A eunuch would be less likely to subvert the king's lover because it is unlikely he would have any desire for the king's bride. And it is certain he could not father a child that might be fostered off on the king as his royal heir.

With how many of *us*, I wonder, could the King entrust His bride? How many of the offspring of our own ideas have been passed off as the King's? God is still looking for chamberlains who will not divert the love of the church *toward themselves*!

As a chamberlain, Hegai had privileged access to the inner chambers, and he understood in detail the temperament of the king—he knew his likes and his dislikes and how and why his favor flowed. Chamberlains were not exiled to outer courts; hence their name. They even had access to the king's bedchamber.

Chamberlains are people in whose presence the King is comfortable. They *know* Him. And He *trusts* them.

A CHAMBERLAIN HEDGES ABOUT AND WATCHES OVER US

Hegai's primary task was to "keep" the maidens. By dictionary definition, the way you "keep" someone is to "hedge about (as with thorns), guard, protect, attend to, mark, observe, preserve, regard, reserve, save, wait for, and watch over" them.[4] I am sure all this and more was involved in keeping young girls for the king. Hegai had his hands full!

This "eunuch in charge" and chief chamberlain was also, apparently, the pageant director and master of ceremonies for Xerxes' international beauty contest. According to the Bible, Esther stood out to Hegai early in the pageantry process.

> As a result of the king's decree, Esther, along with many other young women, was brought to the king's harem at the fortress of Susa and placed in Hegai's care. Hegai was very impressed with Esther and treated her kindly. He quickly ordered *a special menu* for her and provided her with beauty treatments. He also assigned her seven maids *specially chosen* from the king's palace, and he moved her and her maids *into the best place* in the harem.[5]

It seems Esther already had one piece of the puzzle as a would-be bride. As a Jewish maiden, she probably hoped against hope that she could continue to follow the dietary laws traditionally followed by her ancestors. Hegai, who could have been overwhelmed by the dietary requests of women from twenty-three different nations, immediately "ordered a special menu" for Esther. This could only happen if Esther won favor with the chamberlain.

LIFT UP GRACE BEFORE HIS FACE

The Bible says of Esther and the chamberlain, "And the maiden pleased him."[6]

A modern commentator says, "In this verse, the literal translation of the original language says, '*She lifted up grace* before his *face*.' . . Esther modeled grace before the face of the king's influential servant, Hegai."[7]

Esther quickly won favor with the chamberlain of the king's harem, but in reality she was still a powerless woman trapped and intertwined in the destiny of other people and nations.

She was allowed to speak only when spoken to, and she had limited contacts inside the palace as she was confined to the privacy of the king's harem. She had no money of her own. She could not leave the protective custody of the private women's chambers.

How did she overcome such insurmountable obstacles? What made her stand out from the crowd? How did she help shape world history? The difference was that *she listened to the chamberlain.*

There may be many chamberlains in our lives as we move from childhood to adulthood. Esther began listening to and obeying the counsel of her older cousin and guardian, Mordecai, early in her life. She had learned the importance of a mentor.

The Bible says, "Now Esther had not revealed her family and her people, just as Mordecai had charged her, *for Esther obeyed the command of Mordecai as when she was brought up by him.*"[8] Esther in her earlier years learned and honed the skills of a teachable spirit that helped her succeed as an adult in the strict protocol of the king's presence.

> God has this incredible idea that church is about Him.

When Esther arrived, she was just another pretty face among many who were chosen to compete in the king's beauty pageant. (Whether there were 400 or 1,460 candidates, it would still amount to cramming as many contestants into the palace women's quarters as there are residents in many small towns!)

Something made Esther stand out from all of the others, because when her turn came, she alone was chosen as the one to be the queen of Xerxes. As I mentioned earlier, rabbinic tradition maintains that Esther was one of the four most beautiful Jewish women of all time.[9] The Bible also makes it plain that she was *both* beautiful and lovely, so obviously Esther could hold her own in the pleasing-to-the-eyes department.

THE KING CHOSE ESTHER FOR *MORE* THAN HER BEAUTY

Most of the commentators I've read seem to assume that Esther was chosen because of her physical beauty or her sensual charms in the king's bedroom. I'm personally convinced that Xerxes chose Esther for something *more* than her obvious outward beauty. What was her secret? For one thing, she had learned to *listen to the chamberlain.* She intuitively knew that favor comes to those with a teachable spirit!

When we only listen to our own appetites and pursue our own plans and purposes in life, we disastrously detour our encounter with divine appointments.

Once again, as I've said in many churches and meetings around the world, *God has this incredible idea that church is about Him.* Our view tends to be terribly different. We often fashion and orchestrate everything in our meetings to please ourselves, so by our actions we show that we believe church is really about us. Perhaps we can learn from Esther's example.

> Before each young woman was taken to the king's bed, she was given the prescribed twelve months of beauty treatments—six months with oil of myrrh, followed by six months with special perfumes and ointments. When the time came for her to go in to the king, *she was given her choice of whatever clothing or jewelry she wanted to enhance her beauty. . . .* When it was Esther's turn to go to the king, *she accepted the advice of Hegai,* the eunuch in charge of the harem. *She asked for nothing except what he suggested,* and she was admired by everyone who saw her.[10]

Did you notice that little phrase, "she accepted the advice of Hegai"? This simple statement speaks volumes about Esther's wisdom.

The fact that "she accepted" means she probably *asked*!

ONE BY ONE THEY WENT ON THEIR ONCE-IN-A-LIFETIME DATE

The contestants in the palace of King Xerxes were the best and most striking international beauties. Night by night, for as long as four years, these young women went one by one for their once-in-a-lifetime date with the king.

Just before their appointed time came, each woman was taken on a no-limit, no-boundaries shopping spree. The chamberlain took them to the

Persian equivalent of Fifth Avenue in New York City, or Parisian houses of couture, to consult with the best fashion designers of the day.

Perhaps the first stop on the tour was the House of Dior, followed by Versace, Armani, and so on. There must have been an entire train of servants lugging all of the boxes, gowns, jewelry, and shoes. Cost didn't really matter because each candidate was given the privilege of shopping with the king's platinum credit card and an unlimited budget.

"Which dress would you like? *All* of them? Quite nice. Our perfumer will craft a personal fragrance just for you if you so desire, and perhaps you desire some custom-made jewelry to go with your striking gown?" Can you see the young maidens looking critically at themselves in the mirrors? "How does it look? Does it drape well?"

I wonder what the chamberlain thought, watching candidate after candidate sniff the perfumes on delicate wrists and remarking with delight, "I've always wanted a dress this color! Can you imagine what my friends back home would say if they could see me now? Just look at this gold necklace!"

He was accustomed to hearing the excited chatter echo through the harem as young provincial maidens suddenly thrust into the limelight compared their unbelievable purchases after their all-expenses-paid outings. Put this in a personal context. What if you were offered this shopping experience today? Think of it: limo at your door, private jet waiting to whisk you to Paris or New York, silks, custom tailors waiting to serve you in exclusive and private fitting sessions. . . .

ONE MAIDEN STOOD OUT IN THE CHAMBERLAIN'S MEMORY

There was one trip and one maiden that would forever stand out in Hegai's memory. This girl didn't have the giddy excitement or confidence of the others. When he took her shopping to prepare for her night with the king, she just seemed to fumble through the racks.

He watched with fresh interest as she wandered aimlessly from one thing to another looking somewhat lost in the process. The signs of frustration and uncertainty were unmistakable as she held up one item after another and shook her head. She even tried on some of the clothing, but something was wrong. Esther's face mirrored the trouble she felt in her heart as she finally approached her new confidant, Hegai.

She knew the chamberlain had direct access to the inner chambers of the king. He was authorized to enter even the deepest recesses of the palace because he was an official of trust. He had been there a long time and had acquired great authority due to his loyalty. Years spent in an inside-the-palace lifestyle had not been wasted. He was very observant. All of this meant that Hegai knew virtually everything about the sovereign he served.

The chamberlain had seen maidens come and he had seen them go— go to the other house, the king's house of concubines. He didn't begrudge them anything; this was their one opportunity to live a dream, if only for a moment.

ANYONE *COULD* LISTEN— ESTHER *DID* LISTEN

His practiced eye caught the troubled look on the face of this one very special young maiden. He sensed a strange aura of destiny as innocently wise eyes looked questioningly at him.

"Hegai, I . . . I've got a problem."

"What is it, Esther?" (The chamberlain called her by name, as she had made such an impression on him that her name could not be forgotten.)

"Hegai, I can't . . . I just can't pick a dress."

"Well, Esther, that's no problem. We will go to the next boutique. Or I could call the couture designers and have them create a dress specifically for you. Remember, Esther: Budget is no problem. If you don't see a dress that you like, then we will have one made for you."

"No, Hegai, that's not the problem."

(He listened intently as she stumbled over her words.)

"You see, well, the problem is that *I don't know the king like you do*. . . . I don't know how to say this, Hegai, but something in my heart tells me it's not about what color of dress *I* want to wear—it's about *his* favorite color. It's not about what style of dress *I've* always wanted to wear; it is about what style *he* likes."

Suddenly the wise official's heart began to palpitate. He was impressed with this virgin called Esther—he sensed she would heed his advice. *This just might be the one,* he thought to himself. *All of the other young maidens seemed to be interested only in what they wanted. All they talked about was their favorite color and their favorite style. Yes, this Esther is dramatically different.*

DESCRIBE THE KING'S FAVORITE COLOR

His thoughts are confirmed when, in ultimate wisdom, Esther's quandary turned to quiet demand.

> "Chamberlain Hegai, you know the king better than I do. Describe his favorite color to me. Tell me what clothing style he most appreciates. Will you list for me the things that the king really likes? I'm not interested in choosing things for myself. I will gladly wear *what he wants,* instead of trying to force upon him the things that I prefer."

How do we make our choices as the bride of Christ when we go before the King in a worship service? Sometimes we walk into a service and get upset if the worship leader chooses worship songs that aren't on *our* Top 20 list.

The truth is dawning on more and more of us that *we are not the object of worship.* The purpose of church is not exclusively to entertain us or to meet our needs. The chief purpose of church is to entertain, minister to, and serve the King.

More of us need to follow Esther's lead and listen to the king's chamberlain. Esther's secret was that she valued the chamberlain's advice over her own opinion.

Have you ever heard the words "Be doers of the word, and not hearers only, deceiving yourselves"?[11] Esther gained favor because she heard a word from the chamberlain and then she *did* what she heard. (She did more than talk the talk; she walked the walk and allowed God to escort her right into the king's heart.)

If you want to gain access to the inner recesses in the palace of presence, if you long to enter the inner chambers and the secret place of the Most High, then begin with the first step: Understand that it's not about you. Again, *God still has this incredible idea that church is about Him.* Miracles occur when our wishes coincide and align with His.

> Seek out someone who has already been to the inner chambers.

The first step leads naturally to the second: *Seek out someone who has already been to the "inner chambers" of God.* Ask him or her to teach you about the King's favorite color and His clothing of choice. Hegai was one of Esther's greatest secrets. Who is your Hegai?

What were the other young maidens thinking when they walked up to the king's door? Perhaps they said to themselves, "Don't I look good?" When Esther stepped before the portal, perhaps she said, "I hope *he* thinks I look good." Lay aside the robes of self-righteousness and put on the garments of praise! Hegai taught Esther this.

History tells us that whatever these young maidens wore during their visit with the king, they were allowed to keep for the rest of their lives. This even included the jewelry that adorned them. Judging by the extensive collections of exquisite items found in archeological digs in the region, jewelry was very important in the Persian culture.

It is possible that the women who visited the king had rings on every finger and most of their toes. Their ears displayed a dazzling array of gold, silver, diamonds, and other precious stones. Elaborate and costly bracelets, headbands, and necklaces, with other unique body adornment, may have completed the beauty ensembles.

Why do I propose there would be such an extensive collection of jewelry for just one night? Because when the night was over, everything the woman came with also left with her as her personal property.

It appears that Esther had a different heart. Something set her apart from all the rest. I suspect that when Esther walked in, she was thinking, in effect, *I refuse to prostitute the king's riches to my own private inurement* (personal gain or advantage). Too many people willingly prostitute their God-given anointing for the favor of man.

Imagine Esther walking into the king's chambers in elegant simplicity, perhaps wearing beautiful but simple attire with only one piece of jewelry— maybe a simple gold star passed down in the family line to her.[12] Esther's name, taken from the Persian dialect, means "*star*," and perhaps even her jewelry set her apart in accordance with her destiny.[13] Being from the lineage of David, could this be a prophetic precursor to the Star of David? Esther, the Star of David!

> Refuse to prostitute the King's riches for private advantage.

When Esther walked in, I'm convinced she stood out from the pack in an astounding way. The king might have said (in modern terms), "You don't look like a gold digger. Don't you want some treasures for yourself?" I can almost hear Esther's humble reply (in New Testament vernacular), "No, King Xerxes. I am not after your gold, because I'm a *glory digger*. I don't want what you can give me as the king of Persia— I want *you*."

Some people in the church are more interested in the gifts than they are the Giver. They come for the blessings more than for the Blesser. Much as did the crowds in Jesus' day, they follow Him to the mass meetings more for the bread and fishes and "met needs" from His hand than for the Bread of Life that proceeds from His presence.[14]

How refreshing it must be to the King of Glory when someone comes close to Him in worship and says, "I just want You." For her part, Esther knew that the palace was merely an elaborate but empty house without the presence of the king.

WHO WILL TEACH US
HOW TO PLEASE HIM?

Most of us know how to work in the natural ways, but who will teach us how to "do the work of the ministry" and please God? I read that a great leader said:

> He gave some as apostles, and some as prophets, and some as evangelists, and some as pastors and teachers, *for the equipping of the saints for the work of service,* to the building up of the body of Christ; until we all attain to the unity of the faith, and of the knowledge of the Son of God.[15]

Success comes to those who learn to listen to the chamberlains of the King. He has given apostles, prophets, evangelists, pastors, and teachers to prepare each of us for our own ministry to God. The Bible says God gave us these "chamberlains" for the perfecting or equipping of the saints for works of *service.*

Americans have a lot going for them, but sometimes our independent ways cross the line into outright rebellion (all in the politically correct name of "freedom," of course). It happens every time we come to church and say to ourselves, "I don't have to listen to what that preacher is saying. He's just a man like me. And I don't have to listen to what the Word of God says either—it's all in how you interpret it, anyway. I do things the I way I see fit."

That reminds me of all the beauty-pageant contestants in ancient Persia lined up for their one night with the king. They wore whatever they liked, walked the way they liked to walk, and put on their own favorite perfume before they entered the king's chambers.

WE DON'T SUCCEED BY DOING
WHAT WE PLEASE

There was a problem with this picture *then,* and there is a problem with it *now.* We don't succeed by doing things our way to please "me, myself, and I." Success comes when we heed the wisdom passed down from the King's chamberlains about what most pleases the King.

What is the King's favorite color? For our discussion, let me suggest that the King's favorite color is red, because that is the color of the blood He shed at Calvary. What do you think He feels when you walk in clothed in the "crimson flow of blood from Calvary's tree"?

Honestly, I can't fully explain how red blood can take a black heart and turn it white as snow, but it does. I can promise you that the eyes of God capture every detail when you enter His presence clothed in the garments of praise!

On the other hand, if you try to enter His throne room wearing the wrong dress—say, the filthy rags of your own do-it-yourself righteousness—then He won't be interested, no matter how much you prance and dance before Him. That is not what the King is looking for! True chamberlains of the kingdom have been trying to tell us this.

THE PROTOCOL OF PROPER APPROACH

Esther was taught the protocol of proper approach in the royal court and, more important, the protocol of intimacy—the rules of relationship in the king's bedchambers. This could not be taught by just anyone, but only by someone who himself had access to the inner chambers as well as the courts.

The prospective bride of a king must learn how to dress as a princess. Esther did, and each member of the bride of the Lamb today must discard all of the trappings and clothing common to their old lives. The old garments are permanently unacceptable. New garments suitable for the royal courts of the King become our new standard apparel, day and night. I remember reading the words of a prophet who said:

> But *we are all like an unclean thing, and all our righteousnesses are like filthy rags;* We all fade as a leaf, and our iniquities, like the wind, have taken us away. And there is no one who calls on Your name, *who stirs himself up to take hold of You; for You have hidden Your face from us.*[16]

The King has seen them come and He has seen them go. He is searching for someone who understands that the palace is just a big empty house without the King—no matter how plush or delightful it may be. He is searching for a passionate worshiper who is not as interested in inhabiting the palace and enjoying its royal perks as in abiding in the presence of the King Himself.

When the apostle Paul wrote to the Ephesian believers about the "five-fold ministry" Christ gave us to equip and perfect the church, He was essentially describing the modern *chamberlains* of the King. God empowers and delegates ordinary people with New Testament gifts to train and prepare the *bride* of the Lamb for her role as earthly intercessor, heavenly bride, and eternal companion.

HE WAS THE FIRST CHAMBERLAIN

Mordecai was one of the first "chamberlains" in Esther's life. (Godly parents should serve as the first and perhaps the most important chamberlains in our lives.) He acted as a true steward and shepherd by going to great lengths to protect Esther in concealing her true identity from the king and everyone else in the royal court.

Later, when personal conflict with his enemy, Haman, arose, he didn't protect himself by using Esther's influence. It was only when Haman's plot extended to the extermination of all the Jews that Mordecai asked Esther to intervene.

This guardian's protective measures remind me of the way Jewish parents frantically searched for ways to protect their children during the Holocaust under Adolf Hitler. Some parents denied they had any ties to their children, saying they belonged to their Gentile neighbors. This ploy actually saved the lives of thousands of Jewish children because Gentile friends and neighbors agreed to cooperate and adopted the children as their own. (The Gentiles who protected the famous Anne Frank risked death themselves because they helped shelter Jews.)

Modern chamberlains of the King are responsible for teaching us how to move the heart of God. Good stewards teach us not to settle for presenting our petitions at the gate of thanksgiving or even in the court of praise. The wisest course is to present your requests in the place of intimacy. Wait until you only need to half-whisper it. Once the King's heart is moved, history is rewritten and our future is changed.

Even as you read these words, the weight of some desperate need may be bearing down on your life. There is hope if you can receive the secret of the chamberlain. Set aside your needs for a moment and begin to worship Him in the face place.

Praise Him. Worship Him until you enter the chambers of intimacy. When your tears soak the carpet and all you can say is "Abba," He will put His finger on your lips and say, "You don't even have to say it. I know about your needs even before you ask."[17]

> God is no respecter of persons, but He will do some things for some people that He won't do for others.

If you enter that place of intimacy, you may find that even while you are still at church, the answering machine at home is picking up a message. Perhaps by the time you get home, the very thing you've been so worried about has already been moved aside and resolved.

"Oh, but I've been trying to talk God into it for some time now."

Perhaps that is the problem. You've been trying to talk Him into it. Just love Him unconditionally. When your worship lifts you into that privileged position of favor, you may find that He has met your need even before you ask.

God is no respecter of persons, but He will do some things for some people that He won't do for others. This is because they've learned the protocol of His presence. They followed in the footsteps of Esther and learned how to become a princess. Their hearts have been so changed in His presence that all they care about is wearing *His* favorite color and doing what *He* wants them to do. And they have reaped the rewards of finding favor with the King: They have become a favorite—the King's bride, a queen!

The very atmosphere of heaven is predicated upon worship. Listen to the counsel of the chamberlain, for the path of praise and the stairway of worship lead into the King's inner chambers.

I am not the King. And neither is any other minister of the kingdom. I'm standing in the place of Hegai the chamberlain, offering counsel and advice on the protocol of His presence. Begin with repentance and cleanse your heart and mind of every impurity. Fill your mouth with words of thanksgiving that take you through the first gate. Give Him gifts of praise and move ever closer to His heart. Draw near to Him and worship in spirit and in truth. When the King is engaged in this way, He has a heart to immediately respond to your petitions.

What is the secret? *Listen to the chamberlain* and follow in the footsteps of Esther. Then you will no longer present your requests in the formality of the courtroom. Nor will you be forced to shout them from outside the gates.

LET PASSION TRANSPORT YOU PAST THE GATES

Passion transports you past the gates of thanksgiving and through the courts of praise. It may even usher you past every obstacle into the very presence of God in intimacy and holiness. At that point, you have passed through the veil and entered the bedchambers of the King as His bride.

I love my wife, and she knows that "if I can afford it, she can have it." Our Great Bridegroom possesses all of the wealth of the world. We are about to be united in marriage to the King of Kings, for whom money is no object. He will spend whatever it takes to meet your needs and bless your hands. After all, the One who loves you owns the cattle on a thousand hills, the hills upon which the cattle graze, and the gold under those hills.

If you are worried about your future or you don't know what to do about a loved one, I wish I could personally help you. But if you have discovered the secret of the chamberlain, then your thanksgiving, praise, and worship may well be rattling heaven's gates right now.

Perhaps Michael and Gabriel are saying, "Hold on, Lord. . . ."

"No," He replies. "Don't hold Me back now. They found favor! They put on My favorite color. Look, they clothed themselves with praise, and they have adorned themselves with worship. Their tears and passionate longing for Me are touching My heart. I am going down there."

As a New Testament chamberlain responding to a contemporary Esther: "What should you wear to catch the eye of the King?"

Put on worship and wear it well. The King loves worship, especially when combined with one of His favorite fragrances—humility.

Put your hand on your heart and pray this prayer with me right now:

Father, forgive me for everything I've done that displeases You. Wash me, cleanse me, anoint me, and remove the stench of peasantry from me. Soak me in Your fragrant oil and turn me into a princess bride.

I long to spend forever with You. I accept You as my Lord, and I refuse to go back to the farm of the flesh. I want to stay here in the palace of Your presence. Teach me how to wait upon You.

CHAPTER 7

FAVOR HAS AN ENTOURAGE

Purpose and Jealousy Often Accompany Favor

E*veryone* wants favor. We love to be liked by the authorities above us and the peers around us. Favor makes for an easier life with fewer uncomfortable bumps along the way. In terms of a kingdom, we want the King to like us and the other servants to honor us.

"COULD YOU DO ME A FAVOR?"

Cultures around the world understand the meaning of this phrase: "Could you do me a favor?" We generally ask favors of our *friends* or those with whom we share a relationship. No one expects much success when requesting favors of strangers. Yet we think nothing of trooping up to a stranger named God in times of crisis to say, "By the way, can You do me a favor?"

Asking favors of total strangers is not something we do often. Most of us understand that influence only comes with intimacy. A stranger might hold a door open for you when asked, but he probably wouldn't "open the door" to your getting a new car by cosigning the note! The level of favor you receive is probably linked to the level of relationship you have developed.

How well have they learned to trust you? How much attention have you focused on knowing them?

Esther excelled in the lesson called favor because she focused her heart on the king. I believe she constantly sought to learn more about what the king favored.

With careful study, Esther could have learned the king's favorite style of clothing, its color and adornment. We also know from our King's own love letters that He favors the robes of righteousness! Amazingly, our King does not alter the robe of righteousness to fit the person. He alters the person to fit the robe of righteousness! If you want favor, study the King. (I even know what "dress" the King of Kings favors, for wise chamberlains encourage us to put on the "garment of praise.")[1]

Favor will make you stand out in a crowd; it makes you different.

While it is true that God is no respecter of persons, this is also true: *If you know what the King favors, you become a favorite.* Anyone can become an Esther! Anyone can become His favorite—if you learn what He likes!

Even "throne zone" angelic attendants notice favor on people. The angel's announcement to Mary, the mother of Jesus, included the words *highly favored* and *blessed.*[2] Do you want that pronouncement upon your life?

If so, be prepared for "favor" to bring an entourage complete with unexpected responsibility as baggage. One of favor's most frequent traveling companions is *jealousy.*

If you find favor, be aware that not everyone will celebrate your success. The other maidens may not be excited about your sudden elevation to queen. Their sniping remarks may deflate your triumph. Can you just hear them?

"I didn't think she looked nice in that dress."
"That color doesn't even look good on her!"

Forget about the harem gossip; it has no effect on your destiny. Ignore man's opinion; seek the King's face. Put on the garment of praise no matter what anybody thinks of you!

Don't be imprisoned by man's opinion of worship!

Refuse to be offended or held captive.

Worship may be undignified on earth, but it deifies God!

When you clothe yourself with worship and enter the throne room, the King's favor will flow toward you. It is only then that jealous spirits will tip their hand to reveal their true nature. Ignore them—worship Him!

If the barbed arrows of their words don't penetrate your spirit, their opinions can't change your destiny. Go, Esther! Go see the King!

Favor comes with another partner—*purpose.* Favor without purpose is like pain without achievement. It is pregnancy without delivery!

Esther's life as a young Jewish woman in ancient Persia was marked by sudden and dramatic change from the earliest days of her life. When tragedy struck in her childhood and transformed her status from beloved daughter to destitute orphan, she fortunately found favor in the eyes of her older cousin, Mordecai. He took her in as his own daughter and prepared her for a future that neither could have ever anticipated or imagined. Tragedy and adoption combined as twin teachers to imprint upon a young Esther the importance of favor.

> PROTOCOL *of the* PALACE
>
> 6. If you learn what the King favors, you can become a favorite.

When Esther was taken as a young woman to compete in a compulsory contest for the king, she immediately found favor with his chamberlain. Was this merely her outward beauty at work? As I have said, it seems to me there was something distinctly supernatural about her unprecedented favor with the king's eunuch.

In fact, God's protective presence seemed to permeate every part of Esther's remarkable life. Divine purpose shadowed each instance of favor that came her way, moment after moment. Esther quickly discovered that favor is just a refueling point on the journey to destiny. It is part of God's means to a far greater and more important end. She began to intuitively learn you can't linger at a place of favor—*there must always be purpose.*

When she went in to Xerxes and won his private favor, she was made queen of the empire and publicly crowned by the king himself. He also gave gifts to his subjects in honor of his new bride, which made Esther's name a household commodity in twenty-three different nations and 127 political divisions.

At that point, it would have been easy for Esther to "retire" in her newfound life of royal indulgence and extravagant wealth. Many in the body of Christ seem to "retire" once they enter the King's household as new believers. They assume they've got all there is to get and settle in as if life will be handed to them on a platter.

PAIN WITHOUT PURPOSE IS LIKE PREGNANCY WITHOUT DELIVERY

Our initial salvation experience at the Cross is just the starting point on a lifelong journey to destiny. God's *favor* dispensed to us in salvation is given for a divine purpose. Again, favor without purpose is like pain without achievement—pregnancy without delivery.

The apostle Paul used similar language in his letter to the believers in Galatia: "But, oh, my dear children! I feel as if *I am going through labor pains for you* again, and *they will continue until Christ is fully developed* in your lives."[3]

Esther's story is not the tale of a "rebel without a cause," nor is it the biography of a pampered princess with no purpose. Esther gained the favor of the king, but she quickly had to learn that favor came to her because she was born for this purpose.

What the twin teachers of childhood tragedy and subsequent adoption hinted at and what she intuitively began to perceive, her "adoptive father," Mordecai, put into clear, concise, and concrete words for her: "Who knows whether you have come to the kingdom for such a time as this?"[4]

This lesson began during Esther's second crucial appointment with destiny after her coronation ceremony:

> Even after all the young women [*virgins/beauty contestants*] had been transferred to the second harem and Mordecai had become a palace official, Esther continued to keep her nationality and family background a secret. She was still following Mordecai's orders, just as she did when she was living in his home. One day as Mordecai was on duty at the palace, two of the king's eunuchs, Bigthana and Teresh—who were guards at the door of the king's private quarters—became angry at King Xerxes and plotted to assassinate him. *But Mordecai heard about the plot and passed the information on to Queen Esther. She then told the king about it and gave Mordecai credit for the report.* When an investigation was made and Mordecai's story was found to be true, the two men were hanged on a gallows. This was all duly recorded in *The Book of the History of King Xerxes' Reign.*[5]

PURPOSE AROSE WITH A RIGHTEOUS TASK

Purpose suddenly arose with a righteous task in the midst of favor granted to Esther. It would have been easier for both Mordecai and Esther to stay uninvolved. After all, Xerxes wasn't a follower of Jehovah, and Esther was never really given a choice about entering the king's harem. Perhaps she considered the possibility that things might turn out better if someone removed Xerxes from the throne.

Instead, both people chose to risk doing the right thing. It's interesting to see that neither Mordecai nor Esther seemed to receive an immediate reward of any kind. It was Persian custom for the "benefactors" of the king to receive generous rewards and privileges, but the most that happened in this instance was that the event was recorded in his court records.

No one but God really knows why Mordecai's good deed wasn't rewarded immediately, but history tells us that King Xerxes launched a major war against the Greeks in 480 B.C., the same year he crowned Esther as his new queen. Perhaps he was too preoccupied with military preparations and affairs of state to follow the usual procedure before he rushed off to war.[6] Or the matter may have been handled by lower officials and buried in non-urgent reports to the king. In any event, to all involved, it would seem that no one noticed this good deed.

A number of years passed by, and then catastrophic change rocked the top leadership circles of the Persian empire. Early in the reign of Darius, seven princes had occupied the most important positions of influence under the king.[7] An eighth position soon rose to higher prominence. The status quo shifted seriously in Esther's lifetime with the sudden rise to power of a foreign stranger.

> Some time later, King Xerxes promoted Haman son of Hammedatha the Agagite to prime minister, *making him the most powerful official in the empire* next to the king himself. All the king's officials would bow down before Haman to show him respect whenever he passed by, for so the king had commanded. But *Mordecai refused to bow down* or show him respect.[8]

DON'T TAKE ANYTHING FOR GRANTED

This incident would quickly propel Queen Esther to the most difficult and dangerous test of her life. If anything, the book of Esther warns us not to live our lives lightly. Destiny calls to us to walk carefully and not to take anything for granted.

Perhaps God has blessed you with the gift of physical beauty, sharp intelligence, remarkable organizational and management skills, or sensitive artistic abilities. Make sure you don't squander or bury your talents and gifts under the soil of mediocrity.

On the other hand, don't be beguiled into building a career on that gift and *stopping there*. Nothing you possess, and no gift in your life, has been given for you alone. You were created for something much bigger and more important than your own comfort and satisfaction.

IS THERE A SUNSET ON YOUR HORIZON OF SUCCESS?

Interestingly, the narrative of Esther is careful to tell us that even while living in the palace she still heeded the voice of Mordecai.

There is a *voice* in your conscience—your own personal Mordecai—that beckons you from the pages of destiny: Don't stop now! *If you spend all of your favor on yourself, then there is a sunset on your horizon of success.* Esther could have focused on using her new privileges and queenly rank to keep the palace in a constant stir while gathering to herself more power, pleasure, and personal security.

Esther chose, instead, to move on to the bigger issues of living! She would even risk her favor and her life to accomplish purpose. Unfortunately, most of us don't graduate to that point. Too much

> If you move the heart of God, you move the hand of God. One nod from God and destiny is altered.

of the time we get bogged down in the trivialities of life, and our greatest hope seems to be that "people will like us." Our goal should never be simply to get people to like us; our burning passion must be to fulfill our life purpose in God.

No matter how skillfully you manage to move the heart of man, you still haven't done much if you stop there. Artists, musicians, writers, and advertising agencies all depend on this ability to influence humanity. Learn this lesson from Esther: *If you move the heart of God, you move the hand of God. One nod from God and destiny is altered.* Nations transformed, history rewritten!

If you make Him your first love and chief focus in life, don't be surprised when He maneuvers you into unexpected positions with opportunities to influence the lives of people you previously didn't even know. God is searching for worshipers who speak and understand the "language of favor."

While enduring that first difficult year of cleansing and preparation in the king's house of women, Esther didn't realize that she would soon be the only one who had the access required to change the king's heart and save her beloved Mordecai and their people. She likely thought she was simply trying to make the best of a difficult situation.

Perhaps that is exactly where you are—trying to make the best of a bad circumstance. What you may not understand is that your circumstance is your "university of adversity," preparing you to get a graduate degree in *finding favor.*

If you want to become a "favorite" with the King, you must learn what the King favors! There is no greater lesson we can learn from Esther. Her chief concern wasn't the acquisition of favor; it was to please the king. This is what brought her such unprecedented, nation-delivering, and destiny-changing favor! Pure motives and passionate pursuit of the King's face is what will also bring you to that place of favor.

WHAT IF YOU COULD SAY YES AND SAVE YOUR NATION?

In reality, God placed Esther in that position of favor to prepare her for the day she would say yes to purpose and save an entire nation (and change the course of history in the process)! What if *you* could say yes and save your nation? Would you be willing to pay the price? *"I will go—I will work—I will volunteer!"*

God is aware of every need, every minute of our lives, but He moves and works among the nations according to *His* eternal plan and divine schedule. We think we've done well to finish our onetime fifty-yard-dash of life, when God wants us to live and serve as if we are running a series of marathons.

Society tends to admire and heap praise on "celebrities" who splash across the public scene for fleeting fifteen-minute sound bites of fame and glory, but on the stage of life they are just flirty girlfriends, not brides. Why? Because there is no real and eternal accomplishment in their work.

True accomplishment and success can only be measured by God's measuring stick of success: Did it fulfill God's divine purpose for their lives? Did it glorify self, or did it glorify God and help others?

So you've won a beauty pageant . . . what about your potential? Some folks like you . . . but have you changed their lives for good? Did you reflect God's glory by your true words and godly deeds? Were they moved closer to God and His kingdom through your existence on earth?

The Bible says the young Jesus "increased in wisdom and stature, and in favor with God and men."[9] In other words: *Favor comes in two flavors.* One *flavor of favor* is filled with hype and all the artificial ingredients that have distinguished the existence of humankind in the created community. This is the favor of man. It is fickle and unpredictable!

> Favor comes in two flavors.

The second *flavor of favor* comes from God alone. This favor reflects all the virtues and abiding qualities of its divine source, and it is given solely for the fulfillment of divine purpose.

If you have developed that highly successful marketing plan at the office that has won you acclaim, promotion, and influence, have you asked God *why* He chose you, or did you simply assume you earned it because you deserved it? The question may irritate you, but it may also help preserve you from a dangerous error or misconception about yourself.

If you just sold a house for a great profit and are reaping the praise of the real estate community in your city, was it all because of you? Was it purely the product of your own ingenuity and persistence, or was God's favor also interwoven with your efforts?

I read somewhere that "it is the LORD your God who gives you power to become rich" and that *power or favor is permanently linked with a divine purpose:* "He does it *to fulfill the covenant he made* with your ancestors."[10] Once you realize that God's favor has brought you special awards for achievement, recognition for accomplishments, or praise and promotion for performance and vision—this is when the real test comes. Will you cash in your favor for the fleeting comforts of man's praise and commendation, or will you reinvest your life, your favor, and your success in the greater purposes of God? Will you give Him the glory and move forward to the next adventure of faith or simply retire to your spiritual rocking chair to develop a selfish spending plan for your favor savings account?

> Continual favor flows to those who understand purpose.

Here is the lesson every God Chaser must learn: *Continual favor flows to those who understand purpose.* God will continually give you favor in virtually every area of life if you grow in the purpose of knowledge. This is a principle of life in God's kingdom.

The King is searching for people who have been trained in the protocol of His presence. The kingdom of God on earth is in great need of people and leaders who can move the heart of God.

So what if you can preach well and move the heart of man? As the common expression goes, "People like that come a dime a dozen." Why should we be especially impressed by your ability to sing well and sway the heart of man? Who is receiving the glory, and what is the purpose behind the performance? The real question is "*Why* do you do what you do?"

Have you given up your claims to personal power and individual accomplishment apart from God? What we want to know is *Where are those who can talk to the Most High God in intimacy and move His heart?* I read somewhere that Jesus told some would-be leaders:

If any of you wants to be my follower, you must put aside your selfish ambition, shoulder your cross daily, and follow me. If you try to keep your life for yourself, you will lose it. But if you give up your life for me, you will find true life.[11]

"Self-made" men and women cannot fully accomplish the will of God using their own abilities and the favor of others. It takes the hand of God in our lives to fulfill His purpose through us in the lives of those around us.

ARE YOU ELIGIBLE MATERIAL FOR AN IMPOSSIBLE TASK?

I'm reminded of a quote from Chuck Swindoll's book *Esther: A Woman of Strength and Dignity,* in which he shares a concluding statement by a guest speaker at seminary in 1959: *"When God wants to do an impossible task, he takes an impossible person and crushes him."*[12] Are you eligible material for an impossible task?

Step by step and year by year, Esther's natural-born strength and abilities were crushed and then replaced by God's supernatural favor and ability. Without this process, she was totally unprepared for the enemy who was about to occupy her horizon. She had never encountered an enemy like Haman—very few people have, while also living to tell about it. God did not only want Esther alive—He wanted her to *thrive*! Favor can cause you to thrive even under the most difficult of circumstances.

Perhaps before the fateful day, she sensed the evil lust for power in Haman during state functions or casual meetings. But this man was after more than mere revenge for a bruised-ego encounter with Mordecai. It seems clear that Haman secretly considered himself a contender for the throne of Persia, and he would run over anyone and everyone who stood between him and his prized goal. Even the king seemed taken in by his elaborate ruse. Is it possible that Esther was destined by God to save *more* than her own people—would she also spare her husband from the brutal aims of a covert assassin?

When Mordecai told Esther that she needed to go before the king and intercede for her people, she knew she faced a test that called for more than mere natural beauty or man's favor. The problem was that Esther was not

sure her "favor bank account" with the king had enough funds! She was
torn between fear for her own life and love for her people. The only way
out appeared to hinge on her willingness to *risk all.* Was she willing to cash
in her favor for this life-and-death drama?

Would she step to the next level, or would she slip back into the safe
shadows of celebrity without purpose?

> Mordecai sent back this reply to Esther: "Don't think for a
> moment that you will escape there in the palace when all other
> Jews are killed. If you keep quiet at a time like this, deliverance for
> the Jews will arise from some other place, but you and your rela-
> tives will die. What's more, *who can say but that you have been
> elevated to the palace for just such a time as this?*"[13]

What a speech! Mordecai laid it out! Like Churchill speaking to the
nation of England during the impending escalation of the battle with Ger-
many—"This is our finest hour!"—Esther felt challenged, and she rose to
the challenge! Now the full measure of her greatness would be revealed.

Don't shrink from challenge, but don't face it alone either! Rise up and
approach the King. *It's your time!*

> Then Esther sent this reply to Mordecai: "*Go and gather
> together all the Jews of Susa and fast for me.* Do not eat or drink for
> three days, night or day. My maids and I will do the same. And
> then, though it is against the law, I will go in to see the king. If I
> must die, I am willing to die."[14]

Esther knew the value of preparing for her moment in the king's presence. She recalled every advantageous thing she had learned from her twelve
months of preparation. Now she would accelerate the process and compress
the time into three days.

She told Mordecai, "You need to begin to prepare and help me so that
I'm ready to go in. Ask all our people in the city to fast and pray for me."
By that time Esther knew without a doubt that the source of her favor was
God Himself. According to standard Hebrew custom, to declare a fast was
also to declare a time of prayer, where the Jews would pray the scriptural
prayers of their forefathers and declare all the promises in God's covenant.

Three days before Esther considered what she would wear in the Persian king's court, she concerned herself with what she should wear in the presence of the God of Israel. She needed His divine favor in heaven's court, so she wisely humbled herself in fasting and prayer to array herself in garments of repentance, dedication, and holiness for three days. Only then did she move on to the next step, the lower court of her earthly king. Lessons that are well learned in one forum can give you favor in another. The garment of humility wears well in both heaven and earth.

FAVOR IS NOT THE HIGHEST ACCOMPLISHMENT IN LIFE

First, Esther sought God's favor; then she prepared to appeal to the favor of the earthly sovereign in her life. *Favor is not the highest accomplishment in life*—the fulfillment of divine purpose is! Yet favor is a tool given by God to help us fulfill our calling and divine purpose.

I am positive that three days later when Esther dressed herself before she went in to see the king, she knew what color she should wear. She knew what her Persian husband liked. She had a thorough and intimate understanding of the protocol of the palace, and she knew how to gain the favor of the king. She remembered well the lessons learned in that year of preparation.

Perched on the precipice of purpose, Esther knew her next knock on the king's door could be her last. The law of the Medes and Persians said she was committing suicide, and at least one highly placed member of the king's court—Haman—would be eager to assist in the deed.

The previous queen had been eradicated from the palace for *not* coming into the king's presence when asked. Now Esther risked execution for coming into the king's presence unrequested!

Only royal intervention could save her now. She needed mercy and grace—mercy is *not* getting what you *do* deserve, and grace is *getting* what you *do not* deserve. *Only favor could save her.*

Esther was careful to put on the right garments before she entered the king's presence and asked for his favor. Are we as well versed as Esther in the wisdom of worship? Where are those among us who have learned how to clothe themselves to enter God's holy presence and move His heart?

We understand the protocol of man's presence; we know how to stand up before people and say the right words. We say things like, "I'm glad to be here! I'm glad that you're here!" and "You sure do look nice!" We all know how to do this, but where are those who can speak to God and capture and captivate His ear? It's one thing to tickle the ears of man, but it is another thing altogether to move the heart of God.

Pray this prayer with me:

> *Lord Jesus, help us. Raise up people who, like Esther, can move the heart of the King. Lord, we need intercessors in every city, region, and nation. We are not interested in praying prayers to impress man. We have no desire to sway men and women with suave words empowered by the flesh or by the mind. We want to move the very heart of God our Father.*
>
> *Raise up prayer warriors, Lord—passionate soldiers and commandos of prayer who can move Your heart because they have practiced the worshipful art of entering Your presence in adoration and praise.*
>
> *Raise up a generation of Esthers who have learned the protocol of Your presence. Transform us and elevate us into people who know how to walk into Your presence and obtain Your favor while blessing, serving, and pleasing You.*
>
> *Give us anointed chamberlains of the kingdom who will show us how to clothe ourselves properly so we may approach Your throne, speak to You face to face, and obtain Your favor in times of need. Give us the wisdom of worship and the favor of Your face, Father.*

Remember: The kingdom of darkness is not threatened by those who can only move the heart of man. However, Satan and every fallen entity in his dark kingdom fear and despise the threat posed by those who can move the heart of God. Esther learned how to move the king's heart in her day, and the calling of the church in our day is to learn how to move the heart of the King of Kings. This can only be accomplished through passionate devotion and worship as His beloved bride.

CHAPTER 8

RISK VERSUS REWARD

Spending Favor to Pursue Purpose

estiny has thrust you to the very edge of the precipice. Danger lies ahead. Will you push yourself over the brink in mock confidence and hope against all odds that you come through alive? Are you willing to take a leap of faith? Will you dangle your toes over the edge of God's promises and leap out into the unknown, casting your fate upon the faithfulness of God?

Esther's divine destiny propelled her through a series of perilous choices and circumstances. Orphaned and adopted, chosen and promoted, she found herself locked in the king's house of women but still managed to win the king's heart and become queen. You would think that once you became queen, life would be easy. But remember that *purpose always comes with favor, and responsibility always accompanies promotion.*

Once again the relentless force of divine destiny thrust Esther deeply into a new life-and-death struggle at the heart of the Persian royal court four centuries before Christ. King Xerxes had personally led his troops into a disappointing invasion of Greece immediately after his marriage to Queen Esther. Some time went by before he returned to the palace at Susa, and his absence put Esther's influence into question. It also allowed others to accumulate incredible power.

Shocking news shattered the period of relative calm and security that came after Xerxes' return. It permanently transformed the landscape of Queen Esther's life, even though she was sheltered within the private confines of the royal palace. *Her beloved Mordecai was in trouble.*

Esther acted instinctively when her maids and the eunuchs told her the news that Mordecai was sitting outside the king's gate in sackcloth and ashes, crying bitterly and wailing in a loud voice.[1] She immediately sent a messenger with fresh clothing and orders to find out what was wrong.

Mordecai refused the change of clothes but warned of a *new* plot by an old enemy who held the power and the will to kill every Jewish person in the Persian empire. She learned that the crisis *began* with the unexpected promotion of a man named Haman—and it *exploded* after Mordecai's reaction to him.

> Some time later [after Mordecai saved the king's life], *King Xerxes promoted Haman* son of Hammedatha the *Agagite* to prime minister, making him *the most powerful official in the empire* next to the king himself. All the king's officials would bow down before Haman to show him respect whenever he passed by, for so the king had commanded. *But Mordecai refused to bow down or show him respect.*[2]

Who was this foreign celebrity? How did he suddenly become the most powerful man in Persia below King Xerxes? A friend once told me something that reveals another lesson we may learn from Esther's life: *Whenever God gets ready to elevate you, He must first introduce an enemy.*

This lesson is played out in the life of virtually every leader in the Bible.

Perhaps the Lord has spoken to you about a great destiny in your life. Just remember that the more important your future, the greater your opponent! Do you suddenly feel as if you are facing giant enemies? Hold on—your destiny is about to be revealed. If it had not been for an enemy called Goliath, David would always have been just a shepherd.

> Whenever God gets ready to elevate you, He must first introduce an enemy.

Never let the size of your enemy, the massiveness of his strength, or the volume of his threats intimidate you. Do what you've always done. In other words, "Sling what you've always slung!"

One smooth stone guided by bravery and determination can cause your enemy to fall. *Even a small boy stands taller than a fallen giant!*

The size of your enemy is immaterial. Israel won battles over much larger enemies and lost battles to much smaller forces. As a nation, Israel lost a battle against the small city of Ai; but as a lad, David defeated a giant called Goliath.

Battles are not won on the basis of your strength *or* your enemy's size. You win or lose on the basis of your relationship with God.

Don't fear your enemies—no matter what size they appear to be. Love your God—He is bigger! "Greater is He that is in you, than he that is in the world."[3] When an enemy arises . . . promotion is on the horizon! "Esther," meet your enemy!

With one announcement, King Xerxes promoted Haman to the highest office under his throne, and Prime Minister Haman's shadow suddenly loomed large over every Jewish person living under rule of the empire. *What a difference a day can make!*

The Bible says Haman was "the son of Hammedatha the *Agagite*." God did not insert the minute detail of this name just to fill space in His Word. When the Lord goes into such seeming trivialities, *divine purpose isn't far behind.*

WHAT WAS SO SPECIAL ABOUT AN "AGAGITE"?

Something about this new enemy caused Mordecai to stand when everyone else around him bowed down—even though he risked death to defy the king's direct command to bow! What was so special about an "Agagite"?

Some scholars speculate that there's nothing special about an "Agagite." They say, "Mordecai was just too proud to kneel before another human being."[4]

The Scriptures tell a different story. If Haman was an "Agagite," then he was related by blood, spirit, or action to someone named "Agag."

There *is* an Agag in the Scriptures. He was an Amalekite ruler who was harassing Israel when Saul was anointed as the nation's first king. Agag's predecessor, Amalek, had the dubious distinction of being the first enemy to attack the Israelites after their Exodus from Egypt.[5]

The Amalekites perpetrated their vicious guerrilla warfare on Israel for generations. They committed such atrocities that God commanded King Saul to totally destroy them. Instead, Saul chose to please the people rather than obey God. He spared the Amalekite king, Agag, along with the best of the Amalekite livestock. It is here we see the unforgettable passages from Samuel the prophet:

> Saul and his men spared Agag's life and kept the best of the sheep and cattle, the fat calves and lambs—everything, in fact, that appealed to them. They destroyed only what was worthless or of poor quality. . . . When Samuel finally found him, Saul greeted him cheerfully. "May the LORD bless you," he said. *"I have carried out the LORD's command!"* [Then Samuel said,] *"Then what is all the bleating of sheep and lowing of cattle I hear? . . .* What is more pleasing to the LORD: your burnt offerings and sacrifices or your obedience to his voice? Obedience is far better than sacrifice."[6]

> What you don't eradicate when you are strong will come back to attack you when you are weak.

In King Agag we see the link between Saul's greatest failure and the greatest challenge to Esther and Mordecai. Esther is forced to risk everything and deal with a problem that her ancestor Saul could have handled centuries before.

Saul failed to obey God's command and instead spared King Agag's life. When the prophet Samuel accosted Saul, he viciously dealt with Agag.

> Then Samuel said, "Bring King Agag to me." Agag arrived full of smiles, [KJV—"delicately"] for he thought, "Surely the worst is over, and I have been spared!" But Samuel said, "As your sword has killed the sons of many mothers, now your mother will be

childless." And Samuel cut Agag to pieces before the LORD at Gil-gal.[7]

What is it about this scenario that would make a prophet of God react so violently? This almost seems out of character for a preacher! Or does it? Perhaps Samuel had prophetically seen the future and was trying desperately to detour the dismal destiny of Saul. Just because Saul had spared his enemy didn't mean his destiny would spare him.

> Deal with your enemy now or your children will have to face your enemy tomorrow.

Although the prophet Samuel finally finished the job originally given to Saul, it seems that sometime *after* Agag was captured by Saul and *before* Samuel executed him, this Amalekite king may have fathered a son who preserved his wicked bloodline.[8] If Agag had been eliminated when captured, future generations could have been spared sorrow.

Fast-forward several years to King Saul's final battle with the Philistines. David, Israel's great champion and top Philistine-killer, was still in exile and far from the official battlefield because of Saul's unending hatred and jealousy (David had just defeated a large force of still-existing *Amalekites* on another battlefield.[9] Even David had to continually fight what Saul could have eradicated).

Saul's battle turned into devastating defeat, and his three sons were killed. Saul was cornered on Mount Gilboa, leaning on his spear and suffering from serious wounds.[10] In spite of his injuries, the Bible says Saul's life was "yet whole" in him.[11]

When Saul saw the Philistine chariots and horsemen closing in at high speed, he glanced across the field of battle in desperation and noticed a nearby soldier in battle gear. He called the young man over and said, "Finish me off. I'm going to die anyway, but I do not want to fall into the hands of the Philistines."

The young man said, "But you are a king."

Saul said, "I don't care who I am, you must do this for me." As the young man drew his sword, Saul, the king of Israel, looked up with bleary eyes and, with his last breath, asked, "By the way, who are you?"

The sword flashed in the sun as the young man answered, "I am an Amalekite."

What you do not eradicate when you are strong will come back to attack you when you are weak. What Saul didn't deal with early in his reign would later plague David and all of Israel.

Generations later, "Saul's problem," the un-eradicated enemy, came to plague Mordecai and Esther right in the heart of the Persian empire. They were forced to risk their lives to overcome the plans of yet another descendant of Amalek. *Deal with your enemy now or your children will have to face your enemy tomorrow.*

It was Mordecai who saved the life of Xerxes, but all he got for his trouble was his name noted in seeming obscurity in the king's daily journal. On the other hand, an unknown Agagite named Haman showed up and got promoted to the highest office in the land (short of the king's throne).

Isn't that how it often appears: You do the right thing and nobody notices, yet someone else schemes, steals, plots, connives, and then gets noted and promoted! Hold your peace; keep your ethics. The story isn't over yet.

I suspect the first place Haman appeared wearing his new prime minister's regalia was at the king's gate. He wanted to show off his new authority in public. Mordecai's job was to work as a scribe (or king's official) *within the king's gate.* Satan saw to it that trouble found Mordecai right where he lived. Doesn't that sound like the story of our lives? Not even looking for trouble, but trouble shows up at our door! The battle was on at first sight.

> All the king's officials would bow down before Haman to show him respect whenever he passed by, for so the king had commanded. *But Mordecai refused to bow down or show him respect.*[12]

Mordecai's co-workers pressed him to bow day after day. Finally Haman flew into a rage. You can often tell how big a man really is by the size of the problem it takes to infuriate him. When he found out Mordecai was a Jew, he decided it wasn't satisfying enough to kill only Mordecai—he decided to go after every Jewish man, woman, and child—and their animals too. (This should sound familiar to us!) He acted on his hatred immediately. *Ethnic cleansing has ancient origins.*

> So in the month of April, during the twelfth year of King Xerxes' reign, lots were cast (the lots were called *purim*) to determine the best day and month to take action. And the day selected was March 7, nearly a year later. Then Haman approached King Xerxes and said, "There is a certain race of people scattered through all the provinces of your empire. Their laws are different from those of any other nation, and they refuse to obey even the laws of the king. So it is not in the king's interest to let them live."[13]

Beware of the arrogance of trying to dictate and manipulate what the "King's" interests are. You might eventually find yourself on the wrong side of a royal fight.

HAMAN TRUSTED IN THE DICE OF DESTINY; WE TRUST IN THE GOD OF DESTINY

As usual, the arguments employed against God's people were a deadly mixture of truth and falsehood, calculated to produce hatred and death. Haman trusted in the *pur,* or "dice of destiny," to decree the date of execution for his enemies. Unfortunately for him, he hadn't heard the wise proverb that says, *"We may throw the dice, but the* LORD *determines how they fall."*[14]

Often we don't choose the day or even the place of our battles, but even when the enemy chooses the day of battle and carefully plans his mode of attack from ambush, our destiny remains in the hands of our God in heaven, who never slumbers or sleeps. God can't be caught off guard!

Everybody is subject to a bad day, a day when it seems like your enemies have the upper hand. There's a character in the Bible named Job, a man who had such a *bad* day that *bad* news had to wait in line just to talk to him. Job responded, in essence, "I didn't choose this day, but I'm going to remain steadfast on this day."

When the enemy begins to appear, don't stop your worship. Job said, "Naked came I out of my mother's womb, and naked shall I return thither: the LORD gave, and the LORD hath taken away; blessed be the name of the LORD."[15] Job faced unbearable loss and destruction in his life, but he held fast to his faith in God and emerged from his trials with more than he had before they began.

Haman hatched a plan of death, but a cast of the dice enticed him to wait eleven months to see his enemies destroyed. He couldn't wait to announce the news, however, so he dispatched the king's messengers throughout the empire with the *decree of death for the Jews* on the thirteenth day of the first month—*the very eve of Jewish Passover.*[16]

OTHER ADVERSARIES ALSO TRIED TO COUNT THEIR CHICKENS TOO EARLY

We don't know that Haman chose this date on purpose, but if he did, then he forgot or didn't know about the God of deliverance who spared the Israelites from a death sentence on that very day long ago. It reminds me of another and greater adversary and his henchmen who tried to count their chickens before they hatched:

> The wisdom we speak of is the secret wisdom of God, which was hidden in former times, though he made it for our benefit before the world began. But the rulers [princes] of this world have not understood it; *if they had, they would never have crucified our glorious Lord.*[17]

What Haman didn't know was Esther's secret: *He had just plotted against the king's bride.* Once the news came out that Haman's plot had been transformed into law by the king's decree, sorrow swept over the Jews. While Haman celebrated, confusion seized the city of Susa.[18] I read in one place:

> The Esther story is another episode of that ancient war between Israel and the Amalekites, and by every indication it looks as if God's people will be destroyed. They have no king, no army, no prophet, no land, no temple, no priesthood, and no sacrifices.

They are but a small, defenseless minority living at the mercy of a ruthless and powerful pagan monarchy . . . [yet] God's promise to Israel made at the beginning of their nation still stands.[19]

The only weapon in the Jewish people's arsenal was a secret connection to the king. The weight of destiny hung heavily upon Esther—she was all they had. Your life may be all someone ever sees of God; you may be someone's secret connection to Him. You are a potential Esther! Risk it now!

When your "Purim" comes and the day of the problem begins to loom large, realize that Satan has bribed himself into a position of assault. Don't be afraid—it is at this point that your enemy is being identified. Promotion is on the horizon! The day is near when your enemy will become your stepping stool for elevation.

> The size of your enemy is a measure of the size of God's confidence in your ability to overcome.

When God gets ready to promote you, He will always reveal an enemy. This leads us to yet another lesson from the life of Esther: *The size of your enemy is a measure of the size of God's confidence in your ability to overcome.* The larger and more powerful the enemy, the more potential there is for elevation in your life. You can never become who you are supposed to be without a victory, and there is no victory without a battle. The bigger the battle, the greater the victory!

As Esther soon discovered, Mordecai's enemy was also her enemy. When Esther learned about Haman's decree and heard Mordecai's plea that she go to the king and beg for mercy on behalf of the Jews, she expressed her dismay in a reply delivered to Mordecai: "The whole world knows that anyone who appears before the king in his inner court without being invited is doomed to die unless the king holds out his gold scepter. And the king has not called for me to come to him in more than a month."[20]

Mordecai's blunt reply reflected a life-and-death urgency:

Don't think for a moment that you will escape there in the palace when all other Jews are killed. If you keep quiet at a time like this, deliverance for the Jews will arise from some other place, but you and your relatives will die. What's more, *who can say but that you have been elevated to the palace for just such a time as this?*[21]

Esther's destiny was mind-boggling, but so were the dangers confronting her. Not only was her life threatened by a new and highly placed enemy, she also lived in a generally dangerous environment. The royal palace at Susa was not a safe place for anyone, by any stretch of the imagination.

Palace intrigue had stalked every king in that dynasty. Even the mighty King Xerxes was not immune from human malice and schemes of would-be assassins, fair-weather friends, jealous family members, and embittered political opponents.

The most dangerous position of all in that great kingdom was *any place on the wrong side* of the king's favor. As a sovereign of the ancient Persian empire, Xerxes held absolute power of life and death over every living person and animal within his reach or influence. No court, no official, and no earthly power could countermand his whims, wishes, or orders.[22] *This was all about Esther's learning the protocol of the palace* and how to handle the presence of a king.

MORDECAI ASKED ESTHER TO RISK EVERYTHING

When absolute power is combined with ruthlessness and decadence, no one is safe. Historians say Xerxes became so angry after a storm delayed the completion of a bridge during his Greek war campaign that he beheaded the men building it![23] Who could feel safe with such instability possessing such unlimited power? Yet Mordecai asked Esther to *risk everything* by openly defying the court protocol of a king known for his sudden temper.

Esther certainly knew about Vashti's story. The fate of the former queen *must* have ignited fear in Esther's heart and mind (and of everyone else around Xerxes. At the very least, Vashti was banished from the king's presence for the rest of her life. At the worst, it is very possible that she was executed). The stakes in this risky gamble just couldn't get any higher. This was risk versus reward!

The worst of it is that Esther knew *exactly how she would die* if she failed to find favor with Xerxes on that fateful day. She had seen the hulking bodyguards standing behind the king's magnificent throne during official state ceremonies in the royal throne room.

Scenes of light flickering off of the razor-sharp cutting edges of the polished battle-axes held by the king's bodyguards had burned into her memory. The images haunted her because those axes were not ceremonial.

Who knows how many times the guards had to hurriedly clean off the blood of their victims from the axe blades while palace servants hauled off dismembered body parts so that the royal court could be reopened to waiting visitors? (How would you like to be the *next guest in line* as ashen-faced servants wiped up the last traces from an "incident" and backed their way out of the king's presence?)

It was risky business to approach the king's throne—even with an invitation and under the best of circumstances. But Esther would have to defy a standing death sentence to enter his presence *uninvited.* If he failed to extend his scepter, or even if he was distracted and moved a bit too slowly, her head could be removed from her shoulders with one clean sweep . . . queen or not.

The trepidation with which Esther would make her uninvited entrance to the throne room was magnified by her knowledge of Vashti's capricious (and recent) removal. If the king had deposed one queen on a whim over a slight, what would he do to a new queen who knowingly shoved her way into his presence?

Quite simply, Vashti was removed for refusing an invitation to come before the king; Esther could be removed for coming before the king *without* an invitation.

WOULD THE FAVOR OF
THE BEDCHAMBER WORK IN
THE THRONE ROOM?

Esther knew what it was to enjoy the favor of the king in the realm of the royal bedchambers, but would the favor of the bedroom sway the king's heart in the harsher and more formal realm of the Persian throne room?

This was the political power zone, the literal realm of cutthroat politics. This was the home court of the king's new *prime minister,* the one known as "the keeper of the audiences." Haman was the king's "doorway," the official obstacle of state standing firmly between Xerxes and the outer world. Traditionally, he was suspicious and jealous of everyone—especially the queen—who might threaten his hold on the king's attention, favor, and power. (Very often men in these positions had designs on the throne itself.)

To make matters worse, Esther hadn't been called into the king's presence for thirty days. She couldn't be sure of his state of mind at the time. The dreary memories of the Greek wars and the humiliating defeat at the Bay of Salamis were permanently etched in the king's mind. (Greek historical accounts say that King Xerxes, in his confidence, sat overlooking the Bay of Salamis in Greece on a throne perched on a raised promontory as the core of his navy was surrounded in the narrow bay and defeated before his eyes.[24] How would he react to an uninvited intrusion?

HOW DO YOU LEGALLY SWAY OR INFLUENCE A KING?

Those in the know understood there were three sources of earthly power that at times were known to legally and significantly sway the king of Persia's decisions:

1. the law of the Medes and Persians;
2. the counsel of trusted military leaders and confidants; and
3. the subtle, intimate influence of wives and lovers.

Other than these avenues, the king seemed to be virtually unapproachable.

Esther was faced with an impossible choice: Should she remain silent to try to save herself and sacrifice her people, or should she risk everything and possibly sacrifice herself to save her people? She knew the law of the Medes and Persians was *against* her in this crisis: She could be instantly killed if she entered the king's presence without prior permission.

Sometimes natural law is against you—that is when you need "supernatural law." Natural law said, "Peter, you can't walk on the water." An invitation to the supernatural realm said, "Get out of the boat." Natural law said, "Esther, you cannot enter the king's court." Her reply catapulted her into the supernatural: "If I perish, I perish; but I am going to see the king!"

I encourage you, friend, to heed the whispered invitation to the supernatural: Get out of the boat! Move beyond your comfort zone and set your sights on the throne zone! Destiny awaits!

Queens and princesses could die just as quickly as paupers and peasants in the absence of the king's favor, but Esther knew something no one else knew: She had a secret trump card. She knew the protocol of the palace, but she also knew the power of intimacy! This reveals yet another lesson we learn from her life: She was willing to risk it all on her belief that *preparation trumps permission in the presence of the king.*

> Preparation trumps permission in the presence of the King.

Esther knew how to go around the rigid rules of palace protocol, formal petition, and political position. She had discovered the power of preparation and the force of passion. She had already transformed a one-night stand into a lifelong relationship.

Now she faced a crisis of historic proportions that would test as never before the strength and depth of her relationship with the king. Her new enemy and challenger was taking new ground in the battle for the mind and favor of the king—and he was doing it on a battlefield far removed from the royal bedchambers.

Haman seemed to have absolute control over who could enter that battlefield and under what conditions. As the "keeper of the audiences," he was the sole decision maker who determined who was invited into the king's throne room and who was not. Anyone Haman rejected (or passively ignored) could only bypass him by going through the gauntlet of the extended scepter to access the king. This was the process by which Xerxes could overrule the tightly guarded access to the throne. *If* he saw you, and *if* he favored you, he would extend the scepter to you after you illegally entered his throne room.

It is likely that protocol required *advance notice* and considerable bribes to get on "the list." Esther didn't have the time, and no amount of money would lessen Haman's desire to undercut her influence with the king. (Remember that no one—including Haman—knew the queen was Jewish at this point. Haman's antagonism toward Esther was likely limited to competitive court jealousy toward another influential person in the life of Xerxes.)

The crisis left Esther no choice: She would have to go around this Agagite obstacle and enter uninvited at great personal risk. She must take a life-and-death leap of faith through a guarded gauntlet with an emotionally distant king and rigid court protocol on one side and a deadly enemy on the other. Only the extended scepter of kingly *favor* would save her. *Sometimes you must risk everything to become the "very thing" you are supposed to be.*

The queen understood better than anyone else that she wasn't contemplating a casual stroll into the king's court. Another lesson emerges from the crisis of Queen Esther: You can't climb the ladder of faith and stand on the earth at the same time. At some point your feet have to leave the ground. Before you put the credit card down, you have to be sure it's worth it. You must ask yourself, "Is this a big enough issue to risk my life on?" Esther heard Mordecai's warning and made her decision with determination.

> Sometimes you must risk everything to become the "very thing" you are supposed to be.

Then Esther sent this reply to Mordecai: "Go, gather together all the Jews who are in Susa, and fast for me. Do not eat or drink for three days, night or day. I and my maids will fast as you do. When this is done, I will go to the king, even though it is against the law. *And if I perish, I perish.*"[25]

One popular expression in rural American culture says, "Dance with the one who brung ya. . . ." In other words, "Don't change your methods—keep doing what you know works." As Esther prepared to enter the throne room of Xerxes, she told herself, "I remember how I got here in the first place. The first time I went in to the king, I focused on him and not on me."

Esther set out to re-create her first entrance. It didn't matter that the battlefield was different and that everyone else was using other weapons. She wasn't going for the head; *she was going for the heart.* She knew just the right color of dress to wear and what fragrance would do the trick.

(We know someone else who resorted to the "proven weapons" of his first battles. . . . David stripped away the armor and weapons of King Saul in favor of the simple tools of a shepherd. He preferred his tried and proven weapons of God's favor when he approached Goliath, even though the battlefield and the opponent had changed.[26])

> The collective aroma of humility from many is more powerful than that of an individual.

Esther also prepared with humility. She essentially said, "I will not be presumptive." She told Mordecai, "*You* fast; *you* pray. In fact, get every Jewish person in Susa praying and fasting about this thing." Sometimes you elicit the help of others by saying, "Look, I'm facing a real critical time in my life. I need your help right now."

If you are facing a risky situation, perhaps you should contact others around you and say, "You know, I feel a date with destiny coming into my life. There are some decisions that need to be made. Would you help me prepare? Would you pray? Would you fast?" Still another lesson rises from Esther's predicament: *The collective aroma of humility from many is more powerful than that of an individual.*

On the third day, Esther's preparations were complete. It was time to throw herself on the carpet of mercy woven by favor. Perhaps her own muscle-bound guards outside the doors of the royal court begged her to reconsider.

"But, Queen Esther, don't you remember the law of the Medes and Persians? This sort of thing just isn't done—it can get you *killed.* No one goes into the king's presence without an invitation—it is against protocol and all common sense. No one gets close to him on his throne without Haman's okay." Her trembling reply was, obviously, "Open the door, or I'll do it myself."

Satan will do everything he can to keep you out of the court of worship. He'll use every possible distraction, from headaches to heartaches, from weather to wealth—but you have to decide: "If I perish, I perish. But I'm going to see the King."

Esther made up her mind. *She was going to spend her favor to purchase her destiny.* The moment you walk into the court of worship with that mindset, Satan's ability to control your access to the King is null.

> She was going to spend her favor to purchase her destiny.

Three days later, Esther put on her royal robes and entered the inner court of the palace, just across from the king's hall. The king was sitting on his royal throne, facing the entrance. *When he saw Queen Esther standing there in the inner court, he welcomed her,* holding out the gold scepter to her. So Esther approached and touched its tip.[27]

The bulk of the battle was waged outside the court: *Once you are in the King's presence, the battle is virtually over!*

It seems there was another woman who risked everything for the welcome of the King. Her single-minded focus and passion for Him won her acclaim everywhere the King is known. As I wrote in *The God Catchers:*

Will you be a Mary, a passionate box-breaker bearing the fragrance of brokenness? First, you must abandon the crowd of voices trying to steal or withhold worship from God in the name of preserving man's program. . . .

The Father is bending over the ramparts of heaven. He hears the irresistible crackle and tinkle of breaking alabaster boxes. Is that the sound of your heart breaking? An incredible fragrance is filling the atmosphere, and I hear the rumors of His sudden approach.[28]

> Once you are in the King's presence, the battle is virtually over!

Mary *touched* the Lord's feet, head, and heart with the fragrant oil of her extravagant worship. It is not enough to walk into the King's court. We learn from Esther that *when majesty is seated on a throne of judgment, grace extended must also be accepted.* You must touch the scepter. In fact, worship is not worship unless you touch Him!

While working on this book, I suddenly remembered the first sermon I ever preached (at the ripe age of sixteen). Ironically, it was based on the book of Esther and titled "It's Time to Touch the Scepter."

The king's vocal and casual greeting may have been sufficient in the privacy of the royal bedchambers, but Esther knew that in the realm of the king's official capacity as judge and lawgiver, the scepter was a symbol of his power and authority. She had to reach out and touch it in order to receive his pardon from the death sentence of the law. (Yet something in Esther had to wonder if it *would* be extended.)

We *know* that our Lord and King Jesus Christ has already extended His scepter of grace to us. The veil, the door of separation between sinful humanity and holy Deity, has been ripped wide open. His Word says, "Let us come boldly to the throne of our gracious God. There we will receive his mercy, and we will find grace to help us when we need it."[29]

Come boldly, but do not come without preparation. Esther and the church may rush in where angels fear to tread, but the High King's bride should know what colors please him. (Again, perhaps it is scarlet red, the color of the blood He shed on the cross.) She also knows the King's favorite fragrance. (The King of Kings savors the fragrance of praise and sacrificial worship offered from pure hearts.) The bride should certainly know what dress is the King's favorite. (Put on the garment of praise!)

Esther didn't say, "Come over for dinner, but *make sure you bring* your scepter, your signet ring, your authority, and some henchmen, of course." She just said, "I want *you* to come—and bring along Haman too."

Oftentimes we petition God for revival saying, "We want our church to grow. We want power to raise the dead. We want . . ."

We're busy asking for things *from* Him, while *He* thinks it's all about *Him*. We must learn to say as Esther did, "I just want You." (It should be understood that whenever He comes, His scepter comes with Him automatically. When Jesus said, "The kingdom is near to you . . . it is at hand," He was saying it is *within a hand's reach*.)

Esther knew if she had the king's face within hand's reach, then all the power of the kingdom was that close also. Sometimes we never connect the two. This brings up another lesson from the book of Esther:

Sometimes you have to risk everything to see the King—including your reputation. Forget about who's beside you. Ignore all others in the court of worship. Concentrate on the King! Who cares what they think? What does *He* like?

> Esther *risked* her favor to achieve her purpose.

Then there comes a point at which relationship will surpass protocol, but don't try it until you have learned the protocol of His presence. There is a fine boundary between intimate familiarity and casual presumption.

As I've said, my daughters know that for the most part they can press into my office no matter who is meeting with me. That is because intimate relationship stretches the boundaries of protocol. (Esther had so learned the lesson of protocol that she could stretch boundaries that would be the end of others less schooled in the protocol of the palace.)

My daughters tend to enter my office differently and adjust their methods if there is a visitor in the room. They often quietly and shyly sidle up to me, and they are observant of the fact that there are other people present. They nod or smile to acknowledge them. They may want to ask me something such as, "Dad, can I go here?" or "Can I go see a movie with this person?" Yet they patiently *wait for their moment.* Why? Because they know there are other things going on in the room.

Esther was aware of the other things going on in the king's throne room. Perhaps she sensed a thick blanket of intrigue and jealousy. She probably knew that Haman was scratching his pointy head, trying to figure out why she was still alive and receiving such unprecedented favor.

The queen knew about the protocol of the palace; however, on the basis of something even more powerful, she risked everything to step out of her normal realm and intrude upon the king's. She said, "I'm going to prepare. I'm not going in there unfragranced and ungroomed. I'm going to prepare, but while I exercise all of the protocol, *I am putting the weight of this encounter on my relationship with the king.*"

At that point she ignored everyone else in that court and focused her eyes and her heart on the face of Xerxes. Sometimes purpose requires that you resign yourself to the absolute faithfulness of God.

Are you strong enough to risk everything to pursue the King's presence? Do you have what it takes to spend your favor to pursue your purpose? When destiny pushes *you* to the edge of desperation and the limits of your abilities, cast your future into the hands of God and take a leap of faith!

Begin by focusing on Him, and "dance with the One who brought you on this date with destiny."

CHAPTER 9

LEARN TO WORSHIP WITH YOUR ENEMY

But Keep Your Eyes on the King

There are times when you have no power to choose who sits across from you at the dinner table or at the desk of destiny. What do you do when someone who opposes you or seems to hate you without cause occupies an office or shares your workspace, sits behind you in class, or moves into the house next door?

You have the same choices Esther did the day she prepared a banquet for her husband, King Xerxes, and her new enemy, powerful Prime Minister Haman. *She could either focus on the problem or focus on the solution.*

She could darken her soul with views of her enemy's impressive power base and unquenchable hatred, or she could fill her vision with a view of the king. Which channel will you tune in to?

Esther's crucial moment came three days after she had asked Mordecai and the Jews of Susa to join her in a desperate fast. It was on this day that the queen arrayed herself with royal robes (in the king's colors, no doubt) and entered the throne room of the palace without invitation. Let's revisit the scene briefly.

The king of Persia had many powerful and resourceful enemies—even in his palace—so I am sure he picked only the best soldiers and the most alert guardians in the empire as his bodyguards. It is certain they saw Esther make her unlawful entry long before anyone else. In the tradition followed by executive security forces throughout human history, their lightning reflexes were programmed to "act first and gather the facts later."

The risk to Esther was very real. Those trained executioners were commanded to protect the sovereign at all cost. (Most likely Esther was recognized by these guards, but this executive order of instant death could be set aside only by direct and immediate intervention of the king.)

It is also likely they had *already* darted out from behind the king's throne with axes raised. They fully intended to intercept and strike down the unauthorized intruder whether she was a traitor disguised as the queen or the queen herself!

ONLY A ROYAL COMMAND COULD REVOKE HER DEATH SENTENCE

The window of safety could potentially be measured only in fleeting seconds of time. A commanding tone by the royal voice alone could revoke Esther's automatic death sentence and halt the raised battle-axes racing toward her at top speed.

> When [King Xerxes] saw Queen Esther standing there in the inner court, he welcomed her, holding out the gold scepter to her. So Esther approached and touched its tip. Then the king asked her, "What do you want, Queen Esther? What is your request? I will give it to you, even if it is half the kingdom!"[1]

Esther didn't have to wait long. The moment King Xerxes looked up and saw her, she received favor because he "was pleased with her" and extended his gold scepter.[2] The relieved guards were probably flanking Esther when she approached the throne of the king and touched the tip of his scepter to formally accept his favor.

> And Esther replied, "If it please Your Majesty, *let the king and Haman come today to a banquet I have prepared for the king.*" The king turned to his attendants and said, "Tell Haman to come quickly to a banquet, as Esther has requested."[3]

What was Esther thinking?! The King had offered her up to half of his kingdom, and she chose to invite Haman home for dinner! Why would anyone in their right mind invite their worst enemy to a private banquet normally reserved for a royal spouse?

Desperate situations call for desperate measures. In her first introduction to the king, the initial "skirmish" for favor, Esther risked nothing, for she had nothing! She was a mere peasant given the opportunity to become queen. There's no potential downside to that. How can you be demoted from peasant status?

This time, however, the risk would be enormous. She risked demo-tion—banishment—death! Ask Vashti how steep the penalty could be!

Esther would *risk everything*, cash in all the favor she had accumulated, for one opportunity to save herself and her people.

What would her strategy be?

> PROTOCOL *of the* PALACE
> 7. If your enemy is the King's enemy, then your battle is the King's battle.

Most of us would have blurted out our request seconds after touching the king's scepter, and it is possible that in our haste we would have been denied. Satan often wants to divert us by con-vincing us to fight the *right battle* but on the *wrong battlefield.* It can be a fatal exercise in futility for someone to fight for right from the wrong posture.

This brings up another lesson learned from the life of Esther: *If your enemy is the King's enemy, then your battle is the King's battle.* Esther had a plan of attack, and her weapon of choice was a specially prepared and beautifully served intimate gourmet meal. (How many men have been undone or finally won through the back door of the stomach?)

By Persian custom, men and women rarely banqueted together in pub-lic meetings. Under normal circumstances, the only woman who could share meals in private with the king was the queen. (Perhaps this was insur-ance against surreptitious assassination plots.) It was therefore very *unusual* for the queen to host a lavish banquet for the king outside of his normal environment—and hers. It was *unprecedented* for Haman to be included!

HAMAN UNKNOWINGLY STEPPED ONTO A DEADLY FIELD OF BATTLE

As strange as it was for her to invite another man to such a private and intimate setting, I believe it was well thought out. Haman's eyes were com-pletely blind to the fact that he was actually stepping onto a very deadly field of battle, one for which he was poorly equipped. Battle-axes and swords wield little power on this battleground. I am reminded of the phrase "The weapons of our warfare are not carnal."[4]

When your life and livelihood are placed at risk by the threats and plots of other people, or of Satan, will you stand to fight on their battlefield? Wouldn't it be better to move the struggle to another place where you hold the upper hand?

Esther coolly took a calculated risk and moved the battle for the destiny of the Jews out of Haman's familiar political court and into her more familiar territory of intimate favor. She had no control over Haman, but she *did* have *influence with the king.*

Sometimes we try to exert influence in the wrong arena. At one time Esther had no influence with the king or with his court. By God's design and through His behind-the-scenes intervention, she learned the secrets of proper preparation from the king's chamberlain and turned her one night with the king into a lifetime of favor.

Haman was a merciless creature driven by hatred, greed, and the pursuit of personal gain. He didn't care for man or beast. If anyone or anything stood in his way or hindered his progress up the ladder of success, they were ground into political mincemeat.

As a political predator, it is probable Haman initially viewed the queen of Persia as an enemy. After all, she possessed private access to the king that he did not. But her latest move to include Haman in her royal invitation to a feast with Xerxes caused the prime minister's suspicions to instantly vanish under the glow of self-congratulation.

Suddenly Haman began to feel a strong desire to cultivate his newfound source of power and access through Esther. In the thirty seconds it took for the man to process the urgent command from the king's messenger, the queen's "stock" rose, and her "favor" became another source of fuel stoking the furnace of his all-consuming ego.

Ironically, this master schemer had no idea that Queen Esther was purposely moving this battle of destiny to her own home court where she would wield her tried and proven weapons of worship and favor.

In contemporary times, every sports addict knows the edge that home-court advantage gives to a team. The championship often seems to go to the team playing on its own turf.

It is as if Esther intuitively knew: *"I must move this battle to a more intimate place."* It is one thing to face Haman in the argumentative atmosphere of a formal courtroom. But it is a total change of ambience to seek the king's favor at an intimate feast in his honor.

The posture of "worship" *is* your home-court advantage. Don't fight your personal Haman in the argumentative mode; lure him into an atmosphere of worship!

After entering unbidden into the inner sanctum, and with the palpable tension of her *second* life-and-death encounter behind her, later that day Esther was faced with a strategic choice. She would soon sit down for a meal with her king *and* with her enemy. How would she act? How could she use this opportunity to her advantage with the king and against her enemy?

She would return to her first and most important principle of battle for the king's favor: *Find out what the king likes.* It didn't matter what she preferred, nor did it matter at all what Haman most desired. Only one palate mattered at this lavish feast.

By the time this tournament of roses took place between Queen Esther and Prime Minister Haman, the noxious essence of "the farm" was long gone from the Jewish girl who had become queen.

The exiled peasant from Babylon was now the regal Esther, queen of the Persian empire. She had many years of exotic court life, royal banquets of state, and official public appearances behind her. She looked every part the queen! But the transformation was not complete.

ESTHER KNEW THE VALUE OF PREPARATION

Esther was not planning to offer her king some grilled cheese sandwich slapped on the stove and tossed on a plastic plate in haste. This woman knew firsthand the value of preparation. She had spent one year preparing for her first night with the king, and she was still reaping rewards for her diligence then. This time she spent three days preparing her heart and her life to enter his court unbidden.

The pressure was on! Can you imagine the response when Queen

Esther went back that morning and called together her staff to say, "Hey, guys, we're about to pull an all-nighter." I can almost overhear her cooks secretly conspiring with the chefs in the king's palace: "Listen, Queen Esther tells us that you prepare a breast of hummingbird that is so good the king overeats every time you prepare it. He is coming *to our side*! The queen said that if you will share your secrets with us, then in turn we will . . ."

Everyone in the palace must have been shocked by the news that the great King Xerxes would leave his side of the palace for a private banquet with the queen and the prime minister. This was strictly outside of official state protocol. The palace was all abuzz.

When God's manifest presence steps over into our everyday realm and becomes tangible in the church or culture, we call it "revival." We know from history that society is all abuzz when the divine essence of God walks into the human realm.

THERE IS A HIGHER PROTOCOL
OF HIS PRESENCE

This saga began with Esther's intuitive choice while in the throne room, choosing to seek the king's presence at a banquet rather than the immediate offer of answered petition from his hand. What choices are you making when you approach the Lord's throne in prayer and praise? When you enter in, do you struggle with an inner urgency to make your petitions, tell Him all of your problems, and describe all of the injustices done against you? (If you do, I don't blame you. But there *is* a better way, a higher protocol of His presence. . . .)

> Your first and most passionate petition should be for the King's presence.

Why settle for half the kingdom when you can have the King? If you have the King, the *whole kingdom* is at your disposal!

Esther had some very urgent petitions and legitimate complaints to share with Xerxes. But she chose to petition for more time in his presence *first* and to honor him with her undivided attention. She would talk about her problems later.

When the king initially asked Esther what she wanted and promised her up to half his kingdom, Esther said, "If it please Your Majesty, *let the king and Haman come today to a banquet I have prepared for the king.*"[5]

Esther teaches us to make our first petition a request for the King's presence. Move your needs, wants, and fears back to second place. Your first petition must be solely for Him. This is really the essence and central core of worship. God longs for you and me to seek His face, not merely the blessings in His hands. Again we learn a lesson from Esther: *Your first and most passionate petition should be for the King's presence.* "I just want You at a banquet of my worship!"

How wise Esther was: She knew that if she could get in the king's presence, then she would automatically gain access to his royal scepter with all of its power. She had gained that wisdom through personal application of all the secrets she learned from the king's chamberlain.

By this time Esther's standards of excellence—and in particular her knowledge of the king's desires, tastes, and chief delights—were far higher and more refined than they were the first night she spent in his presence. She had begun with the rudimentary instructions received from the king's chamberlain, and she had faithfully planted them in the soil of the king's heart. Now after spending several years as the king's wife and queen, her harvest from those early seeds of knowledge about the heart of Xerxes was virtually unequalled.

When Esther promised to prepare a banquet for her king, he knew that she *meant* it. His quick acceptance of this invitation implies impressive trust in whatever Esther's evening entailed. This private banquet would be a genuine feast for the eyes, the heart, the taste buds, and the stomach. He knew Queen Esther would provide him with no trite cheese-and-cracker snack or finger-food hors d'oeuvres.

If Haman had been foolish enough to ask, the king would have told him to expect every fine delicacy and rare wine known to the discerning and educated palates of royalty. No one knew how to please the king better than his regal queen, *and he knew it.*

Esther had done something right. When she invited Xerxes to her banquet, there was *no hesitation.* Not only did he instantly accept, but he also abruptly dispatched a messenger ordering Haman to drop everything, suspend his schedule, cancel his appointments, and obey the queen's request.

ESTHER HAD A REPUTATION FOR EXTRAVAGANT EXCELLENCE

This kingly husband was not about to miss this opportunity to enjoy his queen's bounty. Esther had established a reputation for extravagant excellence with her king and husband!

What would happen if the church established a reputation for extravagant excellence with her King and Bridegroom? How many enemies, to their total consternation, would He command to attend our praise and worship banquets? Is God eager to suspend the schedules of His kingdom to attend our worship services, or does He rarely show up in His manifest glory? Have you established a reputation in heaven through your worship on earth?

If we asked God to come to our banquet of praise, would He give our enemies a glowing report about our banqueting fare? Or would He say, "You're invited, but you had better stop by the fast-food restaurant on the way. The table is usually bare, and what *is* there is usually cold or old—and the meal ends quickly. That's when the nagging petitions begin."

Esther held the banquet in the "court of the garden of the king's palace." Again, this was far removed from the formal royal court with its lofty pillars, elaborate throne, and forbidding doors flanked by armed guards. This court was a more intimate enclosed area adjacent to the massive open garden, where years before the king had hosted the leaders of the city of Susa.

The decorations for the outer garden were beyond comprehension to the modern mind (and no one really knows how luxurious the hall of wine or this court of the garden was).[6] It is unlikely that anything we have today would even begin to match its splendor.[7]

Despite the impressive surroundings and the splendid feast before her, Esther could not afford to be distracted or impressed with unimportant things. Remember, *the palace is just a big empty house without the king.*

On this day of destiny, Esther would make no appeals based on the law. Nor would she craft masterful arguments based on ethics, political gain, or international strategy. She was *going for the heart,* using every tool and secret she possessed. It is at this first banquet and the subsequent one that followed it (on the next night) that we discover one of the most important lessons revealed in the life of Esther.

EAT WITH YOUR ENEMY

Saul was commanded to battle Amalek's offspring with sword and arrow. David eliminated the band of Amalekites that attacked his family at Ziklag using spear and swords as well. But Esther would soon eliminate her Amalekite threat with the weapons of passionate preparation and indulgent worship.

The name of God isn't mentioned a single time in the book of Esther, nor is there a single prayer offered to heaven in this book. Yet God's working is interwoven within the layers of every single chapter of Esther's book. God working undercover in covert action can be just as powerful as God working openly in overt action.

We often would like God to simply barge in and take over, but He sometimes works behind the scenes to see His purposes come to pass. Nothing attracts God's presence and His intervening power like focused and single-minded worship. The problem is that most of us have a genuine focus problem when it comes to worship. We want to cling to our problems and the past with one hand while offering God a miniature handful of measured worship with the other.

Are you focused on your problems or on your Solution? So how *do you* worship with your enemy at the same table? You focus on the King of Kings instead of on your enemy.

EITHER BELIEVE GOD
OR BELIEVE SATAN'S PRESS RELEASE
ON YOUR PROBLEM

When you focus your attention on the wrong thing, you are actually worshiping it! You are allotting time and faith to it! Either believe God or believe Satan's press release on your problem.

Jesus constantly admonishes us to believe God and act on His Word. He said, in essence, "The lily takes no thought about what it will wear. . . . It doesn't worry about how this is going to happen or how that is going to happen. All it does is lift up its head, knowing that God is going to take care of it."[8]

Jesus warned us not to worry! Worry is not worship! Some people worry on their knees and call it prayer. Others have mastered the art of worrying with their hands in the air, calling it worship. Worship is not worry! Worry always glorifies the problem while minimizing the value, power, and potential of the Solution. Magnifying God minimizes the problem![9]

> *Learn to worship with the enemy at your table!*

Even if for isolated moments of time you could ignore the fact that the enemy is at the same table, you will still have limited results if you do not know how to worship Him with single-minded focus.

It's one thing to view an enemy across a battlefield, but it is much more difficult when your enemy is so close that the death of a dream appears to be around the corner. Worship becomes difficult for many when they know that if something doesn't happen to their finances in the next month, their child won't graduate from college or their car will be repossessed. It is harder to worship with the diagnosis of cancer in your pocket than when a bonus check fills that space. But worship is never more important than when the enemy launches a plot to destroy your destiny! *Learn to worship with the enemy at your table!*

We know the enemy is at the table when we must fight our way through just to pray or praise God. It is a good thing to plan your days and allot your time for maximum effectiveness. It is important for us to be good stewards over our finances. Yet worship remains our most important ministry and spiritual weapon on any given day. In fact, you've never really worshiped until you have worshiped with your enemy at the same table.

DON'T GET DISTRACTED WHEN SATAN CRASHES YOUR PARTY

When things get difficult and the enemy shows up without welcome to crash your party with God, don't get distracted. Above all, don't allow this distracting problem to derail your worship and move you onto its own unfair battlefield with the prideful thought, *Let* **me** *get in there and fight this fight.*

I don't remember God saying that *we* were greater than our enemies, but I do seem to remember that He said, "Greater is he that is in you, than he that is in the world."[10] Deliverance and provision arrive when we become so focused on Him that we can ignore our sworn enemy and worship our sovereign King! Even with a bad prognosis in hand!

Always remember that *the King is more important than your enemy* or your problem. If you have the heart of the King, then your enemies become His enemies and your problems become footstools for the Divine Solution.

Don't allow yourself to become distracted or driven by your problem. Esther could have allowed her enemy to hurry the process or drive her to misuse her legal status as queen. She could have made a strategic and tactical mistake by arguing in the formal courtroom.

CONDUCT YOUR FIGHT FROM THE POSTURE OF LOVE

Instead, Esther transferred the battle to a familiar battlefield where she could make the best use of her proven resources. She knew how to win the heart of a king. She didn't barge into the royal court waving her queen's tiara and try to take upon herself the role of a lawyer or advocate. She said, "That isn't my strength. I love the king, and *that* is my strength. If *from the posture of love* I explain my plight and describe the plot of the enemy, my assault will be more powerful. . . ."

> So the king and Haman went to Esther's banquet. And while they were drinking wine, the king said to Esther, "Now tell me what you *really* want."[11]

Esther was totally focused on Xerxes throughout the banquet. She knew beyond any doubt that Haman himself had planned the systematic murder of every Jewish adult and child in the Persian empire. Yet she was able to focus so closely on the presence of the king that Haman's grinning visage at the same table didn't bother or distract her in the least. *Ignore the enemy—worship the King!*

Ironically, Haman had no clue that this courageous Jewish woman was cleverly arranging his demise at that moment—at that table! This gives a new depth of meaning to the psalmist's prophetic declaration:

You prepare a table before me in the presence of my enemies.[12]

If you learn to worship while the enemy sits across from you at the same table; if you can learn to pay such close attention to the King that you forget about the enemy staring you in the face . . .

Then you win.

There is no substitute for the King's favor.

CHAPTER 10

DIVINE INSOMNIA

Indulgent Worship Creates a Sleepless King

N o one really knows what King Xerxes feasted on at the banquets prepared by Queen Esther. I once read that at a feast connected to Daniel in Babylon, trained peacocks actually walked the length of the banquet hall carrying drinks for the king's guests on their backs!

Perhaps King Xerxes and Haman dined on steaming platters of delicately filleted breast of hummingbird—carefully positioned on ivory and ebony toothpicks, displayed on mountains of brilliantly colored exotic fruits and an endless assortment of spicy sauces and relishes.

Just think: What did Esther have to prepare for the impromptu second night's banquet to top what was served at the first? It would have to be good.

Esther was the ultimate *summa cum laude* graduate of the Chamberlain's School of Royal Protocol and Proper Preparation. She *knew* the great value of advance preparation.

Her preparation paid off. Xerxes must have thoroughly enjoyed himself at the queen's feast, because we are told, "On *that night* could not the king sleep."[1] Somehow she had induced "royal insomnia" in the heart of the king by the end of the royal repast.

" . . . *that night* . . ."

Have you ever needed a "*that* night"? Or a "*that* day"? An epoch-making event. A critical juncture. A crisis turning point. A point before which things were going wrong, but after which things began to go right?

What are the ingredients for a "that" night? What is mixed into the recipe?

Understanding what goes into creating that moment of divine favor . . . this was *Esther's Ultimate Secret.*

She knew how to find favor with the king. *Favor is what happens when preparation meets opportunity. Success is what happens when preparation meets potential.*

Many are the testimonies beginning with the phrase "That night . . ." or "That day. . ." They often begin with fear but end with favor.

Esther's pattern of preparation teaches us how to create *"that"* moment of divine favor.

Making sure that the King doesn't leave your worship encounter hungry is a key part of this lesson. Offer such an "all-you-can-eat" blessing buffet that the King is full and satisfied. Always have more food on the table than the guest can possibly eat! (That is a lesson my own mother taught me!)

> PROTOCOL *of the* PALACE
>
> 8. Favor is what happens when preparation meets opportunity.

Have you ever gone to a late-night dinner or attended a banquet that was so enjoyable that you overdid things in the eating department? I'm talking about the kind of meal where you push back from the table or lean on the kitchen counter and say with tones of thanksgiving mixed with fresh regret, "Oh, that was really good; but I ate too much!" Then you moan some more when you lie down to sleep for the night. I can almost hear the king say: "There is no way I can sleep in this condition. I'll have to sit up awhile. Servant, help me find some antacid or something."

> Success is what happens when preparation meets potential.

God's powerful behind-the-scenes intervention in human affairs is evident in the sleepless night of King Xerxes.

Here we discover yet another lesson from the life of Esther: *Indulgent worship creates a sleepless King.* Can you hear the Persian king begin his royal groaning to his chauffeur on the short drive between palatial buildings?

"I've never seen so many choices in one banquet! I am king over all I survey, yet I have never seen such exquisite food! Everything I could have ever wanted I found on that banqueting table—and things so rare!

"And *then* there was Queen Esther. She just kept handing me more, saying, 'Here, my king, try this. Oh, you *must* try this—I had it especially prepared for you.' (*And you are aware I can't say no to Esther. Her beauty must beguile me.*)

"I can't believe I ate so many of those filleted breasts of hummingbird with extra mango sauce. *I may have single-handedly put hummingbirds on the royal endangered species list!*"

The king was under more than the considerable pressure of a well-set banqueting table. Esther had also prepared a feast for his eyes and heart.

Once more she had been careful to wear what he favored the most. Each time he saw her, Xerxes noticed his favorite style garment in his favorite color; and her hair was fixed in the way he remembered it on their wedding night. Then there was the way she walked . . . and the way she gazed at him in a way *no one else* could equal. . . .

> Indulgent worship creates a sleepless King.

Just imagine the predicament Xerxes faced as Queen Esther, robed and perfumed, guided him around her exquisite but intimate banqueting table. She had presented a feast unlike any other. Not only a feast for the belly—but a feast for his eyes!

He must have felt like the bridegroom at his wedding reception who really doesn't care for the incredibly sweet icing common to virtually every wedding cake. What choice does he have when his lovely bride in all of her beauty and wedding finery extends the traditional first bite of sugar-laden cake toward him with her own begloved hands?

Would he dare to say, "Sorry, I don't eat sweets"? Oh, no! On *that* night, he has no choice. That young man had better put the cake in his mouth and *smile.* . . . Why? Because he can't say no to *her*!

Do you understand that the King of Kings and Lord of Lords *can't say no to you*? That is, *if* you are His bride, clothed in praise and arrayed in righteousness! He said, "Ask, and it shall be given."[2] God finds it hard to say no to you. In fact, He can't if you ask "according to His will."[3]

"ON THAT NIGHT COULD NOT THE KING SLEEP"

The king of Persia attended that first banquet prepared by his unmatched queen and found himself at her mercy. Her beauty, diligence, and skill in anticipating his needs and desires caused him to overindulge. Some may say that all of this is conjecture, but this much is scriptural fact: "On *that night* could not the king sleep."[4]

There is another kingly man with great influence in my own life who has also experienced difficulty sleeping at times. After my sister and I had each married and established families of our own, we would take our families to my dad's house for various holiday celebrations.

Every night we knew there would be a point at which, with a deep sigh of contentment, Dad would reach over and pat my mom on the back and say, "Well, Mom, I'll sleep good tonight."

My sister and I and every grandchild in the house could predict what the next line would be: "Mom, I'll sleep good tonight *because every chick and child is under one roof.*"

None of us has figured out what "chicks" and "children" have to do with one another (perhaps it is some archaic saying from Dad's past). In any case, we all understood the emotion it always conveyed: "*I'll sleep good tonight.*"

What he was saying was, "All of my children and grandchildren are with me tonight. They are all under my roof. They are all under my protective custody and my personal care. Now I can sleep." (By implication, that also means that sometimes he gets *less* than a good night's sleep.)

There have been many nights when I would receive a call the next morning from my prayerful father, inquiring, "Is everything all right, son?"

When I would begin to answer, he would often interrupt, saying, "I *just couldn't sleep last night*—I was concerned about you, so I prayed and interceded."

There is one night my family will never forget. While on divine assignment in Indiana, a tornado touched down in our neighborhood. I woke up suddenly and felt strongly compelled to instantly move my family to the downstairs bathroom. Having been asleep, I had no way of knowing about the tornado. All I heard was rain . . . *and a still small voice.*

Moments after waking our kids and rushing downstairs, the howl of the wind intensified and the electricity went out, *but we were tucked in the shadow of His wing.* When daylight came I discovered houses around me destroyed! Suddenly I heard the phone ring and answered it. My dad said, "Son . . . I couldn't sleep last night. What is wrong?" My reply was, "Nothing, Dad. Everything is okay with us, but the neighborhood is pretty torn up!"

Without benefit of earth's newscast, my dad had been warned by heaven's radar system. *Divine insomnia had caused him to be unable to sleep!* His intercession had sounded some kind of spiritual warning horn that woke me and caused us to take shelter under the wings of the Almighty.

In the natural as a father, I always feel better when I am able to pull my children close in times of impending danger. I believe that since humanity was scattered from the expulsion from Eden, a similar emotion has been felt by God.

In some mysterious way, could this define how it has been since the Garden of Eden for our heavenly Father? He has never been able to gather together "every chick and child" under His wings.

Perhaps this is the same emotion Jesus felt when He looked over Jerusalem with a breaking heart and shouted, "How often I have wanted to gather your children together as a hen protects her *chicks* beneath her wings."[5]

FEELING THE EFFECTS
OF DIVINE INSOMNIA

The Bible says, "He who watches over Israel never tires and never sleeps."[6] Jesus often spent sleepless nights during His earthly stay as He prayed over impending challenges facing those He loved. Perhaps our heavenly King still paces the golden floors of Heaven—*not in paranoid fear but in passionate love*—feeling the effects of divine insomnia.

What fuels this divine discontent? By scriptural context the "watching over" is connected to the "never sleeps." He never sleeps because He is always watching!

Our God hungers for the rare and highly prized worship of humanity. The extent to which He will go pursuing that kind of worship is unprecedented.

Jesus painted a vivid word picture of His passion in the shepherd's parable of "the ninety and nine," where the Good Shepherd leaves ninety-nine sheep safely tucked in His sheepfold to seek and save the one sheep that is still left *outside of the fold* for the night.[7] The Shepherd was *up* all night and *out* all night. One might say that it is for love's sake that God cannot rest.

There is one time we know that God *did* rest, because the Bible says the Creator *rested* from His labors on the seventh day.[8] However, I am aware of no other reference to God resting again until "every chick and every child" is gathered under one roof and inside the walls of the holy city, the New Jerusalem.

Some people call heaven the place of eternal rest, but it seems God refuses to remain in our passive and powerless box. He is more active, aggressive, and constantly on the move than most of us would admit.

When the God of heaven feasts on the selfless prayers, sacrificial praise, and unbridled worship of His children on earth, *it seems a form of "divine insomnia" sets in.*

He "rested" before the fall and expulsion of Adam and Eve. He will not sleep or slumber now. It is as if God will not rest until He has gathered us together as a hen gathers her brood.

I am sure that divine concern and holy care is what keeps the Keeper of Israel constantly watching with eyes going to and fro.[9] But I also believe we can fuel the "watching and waiting" aspect of God. I think passionate, overwhelming worship can heighten God's activity. In a manner of speaking, it may "keep Him up." What do we prepare for God to feast upon?

WHAT DOES THE KING EAT
WHEN HE GETS HUNGRY?

Have you ever wondered what the King of Kings eats when He gets hungry? We know that Jesus and His disciples were all tired and hungry the day they stopped at the Samaritan village of Sychar. The disciples must have spotted a KFC or McDonald's as they passed through town, because they said, "Jesus, we're hungry. We're all tired of fish. Let's go grab a Happy Meal or something"; but He just smiled and replied, "I'll just stay right here."

Jesus knew He had an appointment not written on earthly schedules or calendars. Even the woman he would meet had no idea that God was standing at attention, waiting for that moment. The disciples were listening to the wrong appetite, so they finally abandoned Jesus after tapping the timepieces of temporal need.

They went into town for Quarter Pounders and Original Recipe, while a weary Jesus waited at the well for His appointment. Divine refreshment was on the way, and it passed right by the disciples on the road.

All the disciples saw was a woman on the opposite side of the road. She was obviously a Samaritan, trudging toward the village well with a large pot perched on her head. She appeared to be carrying a much heavier burden on her slumped shoulders than that of an empty water vessel. (Perhaps you understand what it's like to feel as if the weight of the whole world is pressing down on you.)

The men could guess why she was going to the well in the heat of the day—perhaps something had made her unpopular or unacceptable with the rest of the women in this town. Normally, they came for their water early in the morning for cooking and at dusk when the sun was less punishing. When she saw the group of twelve men approaching, she averted her eyes and moved to the other side of the road to avoid them. (Sometimes people avoid church for the very reason they need it.)

After commenting among themselves about the woman's behavior, the men felt comfortable with their assessment and continued their journey away from Jesus and toward the Golden Arches and the Large White Bucket to satisfy their physical hunger. The weary woman continued her shuffling journey toward Jesus, who was waiting patiently by the well.

Jesus gently led this woman to a place of worship. He even told her that He was "seeking" worshipers. To her cynical view, this was perhaps one more man to reject her—after all, she had been through five husbands.[10]

Perhaps this is why she avoided the busy times at the well—to shield herself from the biting tongues and acid remarks of the other village women. "Watch your husband around *her*!"

But by the time Jesus finished conversing with her, she requested worshipfully, "Give me this water."[11]

Jesus, then, by implication, asked her for purity—"Get your husband!"[12] Sometimes (if not every time), God asks a question for which He already knows the answer. He asks it not for information's sake but to purify our response with transparency.

She responded with the transparency always required of worship. "I have no husband."[13]

Jesus unveils her life and reveals Himself to her. He defines worship's parameters "in spirit and truth," and He recruits her, saying, "The Father seeketh such."[14]

She responds, "I know that Christ is coming. . . ."

And Jesus speaks: "I am He!"[15]

Worship always leads to revelation!

About that time, the disciples return with food for Jesus, only to see her startling sprint back to the village.

"We brought You fast-food nourishment, Lord."

The Lord just smiled in contentment and said, "I have meat to eat that ye know not of."[16]

"What did You eat?" they asked.

"I just had a *worship encounter* with *that* woman," He said.

WORSHIP IS WHAT GOD EATS WHEN HE IS REALLY HUNGRY!

Look at the contrast: Twelve professional preachers went into that village, and all they brought Jesus was a Happy Meal; one transformed worshiper ran into that village, and the Bible says she brought "many of the Samaritans of that city" to Jesus![17]

In fact, this is one of those rare instances where *visitation turned into habitation,* because He ended up staying three more days ministering to this non-Jewish town!

It's obvious this village had favor from Jesus. He extended the revival! They met His worship need!

We also must meet His need for true worship.

How long has it been since God left a worship encounter with you exclaiming, "I'm full!"? We are the ones who often want to leave "blessed"! Interestingly, God thinks church is to bless Him!

When we set a banqueting table for our King that spills over with adoration, love, and the sweet fragrance of worship and praise, we "stuff" Him with our abundant worship. Then, "that night," the King of Kings arises from His throne in holy restlessness. He who never slumbers begins to shake the heavens with thunderings of divine unrest.

HAMAN WASN'T SLEEPING EITHER

Why is it so important to note that the Bible says the king of Persia could not sleep on that night? Perhaps it is because Haman, the enemy of the Jews, wasn't sleeping either. The life of Esther reveals a vital hint of what may happen next when *"that night"* comes.

> *What a happy man Haman was as he left the banquet! But when he saw Mordecai sitting at the gate, not standing up or trembling nervously before him, he was furious.* However, he restrained himself and went on home. Then he gathered together his friends and Zeresh, his wife, and boasted to them about his great wealth and his many children. He bragged about the honors the king had given him and how he had been promoted over all the other officials and leaders. Then Haman added, "And that's not all! *Queen Esther invited only me and the king to the banquet* she prepared for us. And she has invited me to dine with her and the king again tomorrow!" Then he added, *"But all this is meaningless as long as I see Mordecai the Jew just sitting there at the palace gate."*[18]

The most dangerous man in Susa went home frustrated and angry. He told his wife, "I'm a big shot, a *really* big shot, in the most powerful empire in the world. But there is one guy who's raining on my parade. It's that Jew, Mordecai. He will not worship me or bow down, even though I deserve it!" (Remember: Often you can tell how *big* a man is by how *small* a thing it takes to frustrate him.)

IF YOU ARE SUCH A BIG SHOT ...

Ever the "supportive" wife, Zeresh connived with some friends and came up with a brilliant idea that would showcase her husband's incredible ego and boost the prestige of her entire family besides. Can you imagine her starting out, "Well, if you are such a big shot, then . . ."

"Set up a gallows that stands seventy-five feet tall, and *in the morning ask the king to hang Mordecai on it*. When this is done, you can *go on your merry way to the banquet* with the king." This pleased Haman immensely, and he ordered the gallows set up.[19]

All of this transpired on the same night the king could not sleep.

There will often come critical nights in your life when you may almost feel the air thicken around you as you sense the diabolical plotting of Satan to design your dramatic demise. It is true that your destiny hangs in the balance at such moments, but take courage if you have favor with the King!

"How can I take courage when Satan is plotting my demise?" What do you do?

Worship! Extravagantly, passionately—worship! (*As if your life depended on it!*)

Worship finishes the story: The same night that Haman was planning and plotting Mordecai's demise, an unseen and divine hand was orchestrating the steps of Xerxes. *"That night"* the king found himself so filled with the queen's bounty that he could not sleep.

I AM SO STUFFED WITH WORSHIP!

Everyone needs a *"that night,"* but very few people know how to prepare for it. We all could learn some lessons from Esther. Just ask yourself:

What if God left my church's worship service so satisfied that when He sat back down on His throne in heaven, He told Gabriel and Michael, the archangels, "O-h-h, I am so stuffed with worship!"

What does a king do when he can't sleep? What does the mighty Keeper of Israel do when He can't rest? We know what the Bible tells us about the king of Persia and his sleepless night:

> That night the king had trouble sleeping, so *he ordered an attendant to bring the historical records of his kingdom so they could be read to him.* In those records he discovered an account of how Mordecai had exposed the plot of Bigthana and Teresh, two of the eunuchs who guarded the door to the king's private quarters. They had plotted to assassinate the king. *"What reward or recognition did we ever give Mordecai for this?"* the king asked. His attendants replied, "Nothing has been done."[20]

Could it be that indulgent worship—a rich banquet of thanksgiving, praise, adoration, and passionate worship—makes for a full but sleepless King? What does our King do on sleepless nights when spiritual antacids like Maalox and Mylanta don't suffice? If there is any spiritual pattern in the actions of the earthly King Xerxes, then the heavenly King of Kings does two things.

#1: HE CHECKS THE RECORDS

King Xerxes said, "Bring the court records. If you begin to read those boring court records to me, that should put me to sleep. In fact, that ought to put *anybody* to sleep."

(We know the King of Kings keeps extensive records. He keeps track of every cold cup of water given to His earthly servants, He tracks the birth and death of every bird ever created, and He even records the hairs lost each day in countless receding hairlines from every aging human on this planet!)

I'm sure the sleepy chamberlain went through several pages or volumes filled with the Persian equivalents of the legal terms "wherefore, whyfor, and whereas" in redundant rows of sleep-inducing verbosity.

But not even the mundane monotony of court records could lure the king into sleep. His bloated belly just wouldn't allow it. Then the servant spoke words that hit the proverbial jackpot.

Sometime during that sleepless night, the king of Persia suddenly shook off his drowsiness and sat bolt upright in his royal bed. As the weary chamberlain drearily droned on about proceedings recorded from the throne room, something he said captured the king's attention with fresh urgency.

> "Wait a minute! Read that paragraph again . . . the one about Mordecai the Jew."
> "Yes sir."

> In those records he discovered an account of how Mordecai had exposed the plot of Bigthana and Teresh, two of the eunuchs who guarded the door to the king's private quarters. They had plotted to assassinate the king. "What reward or recognition did we ever give Mordecai for this?" the king asked. His attendants replied, "Nothing has been done."[21]

As the chamberlain read the record again, the king realized that a man who had literally risked all to save his life had gone unrewarded. Even in the politically charged climate of the Persian court, such loyal service was always generously rewarded.

All of those things that you thought no one noticed . . . that cup of water, the small but sacrificial offering, the assistance given to a stranger . . .

I seem to remember reading somewhere that "God is not unfair. He will not forget how hard you have worked for him and how you have shown your love to him."[22] Faithful service is highly regarded by the King of Kings.

Nothing you've done has been overlooked. Reward delayed is not reward denied!

#2: HE PLANS YOUR REWARD

Once King Xerxes discovered the oversight, he immediately began to plan Mordecai's reward. After the king apparently stayed awake all night pondering these matters, who should arrive at that early-morning hour but the arrogantly cheerful Haman, entering the king's court on a mission of murder and personal revenge *against* Mordecai.

God launched His own plan of divine irony as Persia's monarch suddenly called for any available high-ranking noble to help him plan a suitable reward for Mordecai.

> "Who is that in the outer court?" the king inquired. Now, as it happened, Haman had just arrived in the outer court of the palace to ask the king to hang Mordecai from the gallows he had prepared. So the attendants replied to the king, "Haman is out there."
>
> "Bring him in," the king ordered.
>
> So Haman came in, and the king said, "What should I do to honor a man who truly pleases me?" Haman thought to himself, *"Whom would the king wish to honor more than me?"* So he replied, "If the king wishes to honor someone, he should bring out one of the king's own royal robes, as well as the king's own horse with a royal emblem on its head. Instruct one of the king's most noble princes to dress the man in the king's robe and to lead him through the city square on the king's own horse. Have the princes shout as they go, 'This is what happens to those the king wishes to honor!'"[23]

Haman didn't know it, but he spoke prophetically when he blurted out all of the rewards he felt he so richly deserved for himself. It must have taken all of the self-control he could muster *not* to insert the "I" and "me" in place of the anonymous "someone" and "those" in his grand speech. If we could hear what Haman really thought while he was talking to the king, we would hear him say:

> "*I* want the king's robes draped around *my* deserving shoulders. Then *I* want to be mounted on the king's own horse (it should really be *mine* anyway). And let the fools who think they actually match *my* measure lead *me* around the city like lowly servants, shouting aloud *my* high rank and praiseworthiness!"

What Haman is really saying is, "I want to be king!" Another usurper named Lucifer once said something similar!

Imagine the swelling pride and explosion of ego that flooded Haman's dark soul in that moment! He was on top of the world, and his plot of ultimate revenge couldn't be sweeter (or so he thought). But what Haman did not know was that the day of divine reversal was about to dawn.

Interestingly, neither Mordecai nor Esther were aware that the tide had turned in their favor. Perhaps, unknown to you, a divine reversal has begun in the court of heaven. Take this lesson from Esther: *Never underestimate the power of favor.*

The enemies of God *and* of the people of His purpose should never forget—it is dangerous to attack those who have favor with the King. Haman was about to experience the unmatched pain of God's justice: a complete reversal of fortunes in the time it takes for the king to utter one fateful command.

> Never underestimate the power of favor.

> "Excellent!" the king said to Haman. "Hurry and get the robe and my horse, and *do just as you have said* for *Mordecai the Jew,* who sits at the gate of the palace. Do not fail to carry out *everything you have suggested.*"[24]

How long has it been since God has left a service or stepped away from your private times together and found Himself (metaphorically speaking) unable to sleep because you so stuffed Him with a banquet of worship?

Such banquets don't begin with a list of our own preferences, needs, or wants. If Esther has taught us anything, she teaches that it is not what *we* want—it is what *He* wants! Meet the needs of the King!

Most of us will encounter difficult days or overwhelming crises when we need a "that night." Not just any night will do; we need a "that night" or a "that day" to set in motion the intervening favor of a King who never forgets.

In moments of despair we must remember this vital lesson from Esther: *Indulgent worship creates a sleepless King.*

Deliverance doesn't come from our own virtues or works; it comes when our worship and love produce *divine insomnia.*

Why should you worry all through the night of human existence if your King is staying up and working the night shift to plan your reward?

The same night that Satan plans your demise, your King is planning your reward! The King who never sleeps!

(*As for Haman, he was happy when he left the first banquet; but things would certainly be different when he left the second. The forces of divine reversal had been unloosed, and nothing would remain the same.*)

CHAPTER 11

RIGHT QUESTION, WRONG TIME

Don't Ask Him Now

Some people can breeze through the book of Esther in one reading and lay it down thinking, *That was a nice story.* Others (like myself) get immersed in one intriguing subplot after another.

One of the most arresting points for me in Esther's story began in the throne room and mesmerized me all the way to the end. This point marks yet another lesson from the life of Queen Esther: *Timing is everything.*

This truth really becomes obvious at the end of the first banquet.

> And while they were drinking wine, the king said to Esther, "Now tell me what you really want. What is your request? I will give it to you, even if it is half the kingdom!"
>
> Esther replied, "This is my request and deepest wish. If Your Majesty is pleased with me and wants to grant my request, please come with Haman tomorrow to the banquet I will prepare for you. *Then tomorrow* I will explain what this is all about."[1]

This was the *second time* Queen Esther demurred after Xerxes offered her up to half of his kingdom. The first time she sidestepped the real issue was in her unbidden entrance to the throne room. Why does she continue to turn down an offer for up to "half the kingdom"? Who wouldn't want half of the Persian empire? Perhaps someone with a death sentence hanging over her head, someone who sees a dark cloud of ethnic cleansing drawing closer and closer to her people—half measures and half kingdoms simply wouldn't do. Why should Esther settle for half the kingdom when she could influence the whole kingdom? *Timing was the key.*

Something about the exchange between queen and king spoke to me as a *husband.* Something seemed vaguely familiar to me in the way the queen was responding to King Xerxes in the throne room. It seemed to me that Esther was reacting according to her knowledge of his mood swings.

At first I couldn't pinpoint what it was, but then I remembered some events in my long and colorful history with my beautiful wife and daughters. That was when I *knew*.

If you don't mind, I'll try to describe it in more contemporary terms and from the standpoint of a husband and father. (If you are a wife and mother, then you understand what I am about to say *far better* than I do!)

Let me pose this question to every married gentleman reading this book: "Sir, have you ever had thunderclouds arise on your matrimonial peace? Where you could tell that something was wrong, but you had no clue what you did to bring on the storm?"

Very often men throw in the towel too quickly and revert to the typically male approach to problem solving and investigation: they go in with a direct and head-on approach. This is usually a big mistake.

What happens when a husband walks up to the love of his life and says, "Honey, what's wrong?" It is at this point, I suspect, that we may glimpse the unseen stratagem and superior modus operandi of the female of our species.

First, the unsuspecting man's wife "checks him out." In some mysterious way, a wife is able at a glance to essentially "take the temperature" of her husband to discover if he is even at the point where she can tell the man what is wrong. (The picture of a partially cooked roast sliding back into the oven comes to mind here.)

> Timing is everything.

In my experience, the first answer to the masculine question "Is anything wrong?" seems to be virtually universal: *"Nothing."*

You *know* that response isn't truthful, but it's as if God doesn't hold it against wives for some reason! I don't know how it works or how it came to pass, but God and women seem to have a special arrangement or dispensation for this sort of thing.

For reasons unknown to me, even the second round of such marital exchanges typically includes some form of "legal spousal deception."

If you say with an increased urgency and even greater sincerity, "Now, honey, tell me what's wrong," then in most cases you will still get a repeat performance of the first round:

"Nothing."

As far as I can tell, what that really means is:

"Big boy, you are not ready to hear what I'm going to tell you!"

Hence, *nothin'*, which really means, *somethin'*.

Extremely persistent or hardheaded husbands can rarely resist a weaker third attempt: "Honey, what's wrong?"

"Nothin'."

You *know* there has to be *something*! You may wrack your brain all day long trying to figure it out. *What did I do? What did I forget? What did I say? What did I not say? I know there's something. . . .*

LIFE IN THE REFRIGERATOR

There is a distinct chill in the atmosphere all day, and living another twenty-four hours in the marital refrigerator isn't very appealing. This means you must try to work the conversation around so you can bring up the subject that afternoon. The same process takes place once again.

You ask what is wrong. She checks you out.

"Nothin'."

The prevailing wisdom in the male community (and some ladies claim this is an oxymoron in and of itself) is totally unanimous on one point: If a wife says "nothin'" on two occasions, then something is seriously wrong.

After that, the range of counsel varies widely (according, I suppose, to differing personal experiences). Some will tell you, "Call the minister. Call the intercessors!"

Others take on a serious pastoral appearance and say, in all gravity, "Go ahead, right now, and set up a counseling appointment."

The oldest married witnesses get a wry look on their faces as they offer the tongue-in-cheek counsel: "Make funeral arrangements." Any way you look at it, somebody is in trouble.

Seriously, when a husband gets that "nothin'" response, it does *not* mean that everything is all right. *Something definitely isn't.*

What it means is, in the wife's mind, the husband is not ready to receive the information she has. He isn't yet "ripe for the plucking." If his wife is merciful enough to spell it out, she might say, "You are not *ready* for me to tell you *what you need to hear*. I will have to work on you some more."

(Who was the first man with the foolhardy audacity to label the female the "weaker sex"?)

ESTHER GAVE HIM THE ANCIENT PERSIAN EQUIVALENT OF "NOTHIN'"

When Esther walked into the king's court, he warmly welcomed her and extended his scepter toward her. That was nice, but when he asked her what was wrong and promised her up to half the kingdom, all he received in turn was the ancient Persian equivalent of "Nothin'."

Esther did add one additional comment: "I just want you to have dinner with me. I am going to prepare a special dinner . . . and you can bring Haman."

The king took the bait and attended the exclusive banquet that night (after jerking Haman out of his normal daily routine, on short notice, with the executive order to appear in his best tux and tails).

It was a big event, and the dinner was wonderful, but this husband (who ruled twenty-three nations on the side) knew *something* was wrong (and perhaps he was hoping it didn't have anything to do with him!).

As a man, as a husband for more than twenty-five years, and as the father of three wonderfully complex young ladies, I'm convinced that women, in general, think men are pitiful. They are convinced that we don't know what they are doing most of the time. Actually, the truth is *more pitiful than that.* We know exactly what they're doing—*we just enjoy the process!*

THERE IS A PROTOCOL OF PETITION

My middle daughter learned how to operate in this "Esther anointing" a few years ago. Her mother—my wife—instructed her in this secret art. It sounds wonderful, and I suppose it is . . . from her point of view. My problem is that I was the target of her petition.

I've shared this sad story of masculine capitulation in other places, and even in another book I've written, but it deserves a retelling here because of its extremely appropriate lesson taken from the story of Esther.

On this occasion, my daughter wanted permission regarding something. When she asked me, I told her no. She shares the collective knowledge of other children across the globe in that she knows how to "shop for permission." She immediately turned from me to ask her mother the same question!

Just in case you haven't discerned the form of this conspiracy, it goes like this: First, you ask one parent. Then, if you don't get what you want, you immediately ask the other parent. If you still don't receive your petition, then you appeal to a higher court—*the grandparents.*

After I said no, my daughter went to her mom with the same request. Her mother put down her dish towel and said, "Let me tell you how to get your way with your dad." (*Remember, I was still in the same room!*) I knew these lessons took place, but at least I'd hoped they would preserve my dignity by conducting the course on the protocol of persuasion *privately.*

My wife instructed, "You don't just walk up to your dad and demand something. Before you even ask anything, you put your arms around him. Give him kisses and tell him, 'I love you, Daddy.' Be persistent! Then you watch his mouth. . . ."

(I couldn't believe what I was hearing!)

"When he smiles, then you ask."

I was sure my daughter would wait a couple of days or maybe a couple of weeks before she tried these new techniques on me—after all, again, I was right there in the room with her when she received her lesson.

That girl didn't wait even two minutes! She went from that "private" tutorial lesson directly across the room and put her arms around me. Then she said, "I love you, Daddy [kiss]. You are the bestest daddy [kiss]."

Throughout the spectacle, I was telling her, "I know what you are doing. . . ."

She would not be deterred.

THE MOMENT SHE SAW IT,
SHE POUNCED

"I love you, Daddy [kiss]." She hugged me, smiled at me, and told me over and over again just how wonderful I was. Meanwhile, I was saying to myself (through gritted teeth and tight lips), *I will not smile. I will not smile.* But one tiny corner of my mouth traitorously betrayed me and twitched upward slightly. The moment she saw it, she pounced.

My daughter asked me the *same question* she had asked not ten minutes before.

With steely resolve, I opened my mouth to say *no* . . . but *yes* came out anyway!

It was the *same question*. You would normally expect the same answer! The only difference was *protocol*! Learning how to handle Dad.

Centuries before my daughter learned how to make her petition the right way at the right time, Queen Esther was careful to prioritize the king's presence and place a higher value on being with him than on seeking a favor or decree from his hand.

Esther desperately needed the help of Xerxes to save the lives of all the Jews under the control of the Persian empire, but she knew the danger of asking the *right question* at the *wrong time*. *Wisdom is learning the right time to ask the right question.* Learn how to handle the King's presence.

THERE IS A PROTOCOL
TO ENTERING HIS PRESENCE

There is a protocol to entering His presence. On a lower plain, Queen Esther understood that banqueting the king of Persia was not bribery. What can you give to a king who owns everything? He is impervious to bribery. Besides that, none of the goods or articles of value that Esther possessed could even begin to match what he already had. And whatever she did have at her disposal came from him, anyway! What *can* we offer the King of Kings?

The greatest levels of privileged access in any royal house are reserved for those individuals who have intimate relationships with the king, such as the queen, a royal son or daughter, other family members, and loyal servants.

A certain spiritual intuition often comes with intimacy. We see it progressively revealed in Queen Esther's life. She had every logical reason to be confident after her triumphant, unannounced "courtroom" appearance when King Xerxes extended his royal scepter to her.

A CERTAIN SPIRITUAL INTUITION OFTEN COMES WITH INTIMACY

He promised to give her up to half of his kingdom, but that *intimate intuition* led the queen to prepare two feasts and twice defer her request before she sensed it was time to tell the king what was *really* wrong.

Sometimes we rush into church and push through our planned religious activities so we can throw our requests at God like ungrateful children, pawing for His hands and digging through His infinite pockets for private treasure.

The victory we seek, the help we long for, the miracle we desperately beg Him to perform—it isn't wrong to want these things. Nor is it wrong to ask or petition the King for them.

> Petition from the position of intimate relationship.

Esther teaches us there is an even better way: Learn how to enter the King's presence and *petition from the position of intimate relationship.* This is far more effective than petitioning Him on the basis of some biblical (legal) point or formal platform in the outer court.

Esther's way is the highest way. In fact, her way was even better than the familiar requests of those welcomed into the king's royal presence as members of the king's court. She wasn't limited to the throne room—she presented her petitions from behind the veil, in the secret place.

Esther had learned the protocol of the presence. You can't just come running into God's presence, point at a Scripture reference, and shout, "Okay, God—I demand this!"

This was the attitude of the prodigal son. At that time it was the custom for children to receive their inheritance when they came of age rather than after a parent had died. The prodigal son pointed to the letter of the law and demanded of his father, "Give me what is mine—right now." So the father gave his son the blessing and watched him abandon the "blesser." He abused the blessings by using them to pay for his ticket away from his father.

If you think about it, this greedy heir disregarded the protocol of the heart and used legal protocol to snatch his blessing from his father's hand early. He used the products from his father's hands to underwrite his flight from his father's face.

How often do we use the Blesser's blessings to finance our journey away from His heart and face? What if this younger son had said, "I just want you, Father," instead of "Give me what's mine"?

What if we did the same thing?

THERE IS A PLACE OF INTIMACY IN THE HOLY SPIRIT WHERE WE DON'T EVEN HAVE TO ASK FOR THINGS

We have a hint of what the father's reaction might have been. He told the older brother, who remained at home, "Look, dear son, you and I are very close, and *everything* I have is yours."[2]

I believe *there is a place of intimacy in the Holy Spirit where we don't even have to ask for things.* Scripture says, "Your Father knows exactly what you need even before you ask him!"[3]

King Xerxes asked, "Esther, what do you want?" and she prioritized his presence by saying, "Nothing." Read into her reply, "no-*thing.*"

"Just come eat dinner with me one more time. I don't want things, I just want you."

Why should you settle for half the kingdom when you can have the King? When we begin to understand the protocol of His presence, we learn how to put Him first, serve Him first, and please Him first. Those who know the right time and the right place to make their requests will see those things come to pass *in greater fullness and with greater effect.*

Petition from the position of intimate relationship! Don't forget the first principle: You must *be* in relationship. Seek His face with "I love You, Daddy!" and watch for His smile!

Most children understand this process instinctively (and then forget it later in life). When my youngest daughter was about six, she was a master of the art of gentle persuasion. One time I came home from a trip and sat down in my favorite chair to read the paper.

My daughter knew this was one my favorite ways to relax, but she had something more important to communicate than merely the news of the day.

Just as soon as I had the paper folded and positioned just right, she jumped up in my lap and pushed the paper out of the way. Then she did what no one outside of my family can do: *she took my face in her hands to direct my gaze.*

"I love you, Dad."

"I love you too. Let me read my paper."

"I love you, Dad."

"I love you too."

Sensing that my paper would remain on the floor until I finally gave in to this irresistible force, I sighed in mock irritation and said, "Okay, honey. What do you want?"

"Nothin'. I just want you."

SHE WANTS SOMETHING REALLY BIG

That is when I thought to myself, *She wants something really big.* I couldn't resist throwing out the fishing line just one more time, so I started reading my paper as if nothing had happened, even though it was difficult with a lap full of very determined daughter.

"I love you, Dad." [Kiss, kiss, kiss, kiss.] It was getting really serious at this point.

"What do you *really* want, honey?"

"I just miss you, Dad." I could feel dollars pouring out of my pocket already. I *knew* she wanted something, but she was too wise in persuasive years to release her request too soon. She just kept throwing me off balance by saying, "I don't want anything—I just want you."

It wasn't long before that little girl melted my heart. When I couldn't take the strain any longer, I asked my wife, "How long before dinner?"

She said, "About an hour."

I turned to my daughter and said, "Come on, baby, let's go." We drove into town and pulled up in front of a toy store. Keep in mind that my daughter hadn't asked for anything, but by the time she finished loving on me, I wanted to walk in the toy store and say right out loud, "Which *half* of the store do you want? This half or that half?"

SHE LEGITIMATELY WOOED ME BY SEEKING MY FACE

Why? It was because my little girl had legitimately wooed me by seeking my face, not my hands.

Retrace the steps Esther took to the point of petition with the king:

The day the king spared the queen's life in the throne room:
"Esther, what do you want?"
"I just want you. I just want to spend time with you."
"Esther, whatever you want, I'll give it to you—up to half of my kingdom" (Haman must have been startled at this remark).
"Just come and eat dinner with me today—and bring your buddy Haman."

Later that evening:
At the end of the first banquet, the king asks Esther a second time to tell him what's wrong. He knows something is up, but he sure is enjoying the process of finding out.
"Esther, honestly, what do you want? I'm serious now."
"I just want you. I just want to spend time with you."
"Esther, whatever you want, I'll give it to you—up to half of my kingdom." (Haman could see his private plans for the kingdom slipping away in an avalanche of kingly romantic feelings toward Esther. *But it sure is good to know that I am such a favorite*

with the queen, he thought smugly to himself, although he wondered why he had felt somewhat ignored all night.)

The king persisted: "Tell me what you really want, Esther."

"No, you are *still* not . . . er, *I* am still not ready to tell you. But . . . come to another banquet I've prepared for you tomorrow—and Haman is invited too. Let me serve you first in another feast of abundance. *Then* I will tell you my heart's desire."

STUFFED WITH ABUNDANCE, ENAMORED BY BEAUTY, AND READY TO LISTEN

It is at this point of incredible anticipation that Esther leaves Xerxes so stuffed with the abundance of her banquet, so enamored by her beauty, and so eager to hear her request that he cannot sleep. As we learned earlier, *indulgent worship creates a sleepless King.*

When the King "works the night shift with you in mind," destinies are raised from the ashes of evil plots, and high strategies of destruction against good people are struck down. Perhaps Queen Esther slept like a baby through the night, while King Xerxes paced the floor with insomnia (and Haman burned the midnight oil, planning and anticipating his bitter revenge).

If we can ever refine our pursuit to the point where we genuinely value the King more than the kingdom, we'll be amazed to discover what the King will do for us. Remember: Seek the heart of the King, not the splendor of the kingdom.

The morning sun would rise on a new landscape, *a day of divine reversals* and changes of fortune totally beyond the wildest imaginations of men. (I remember reading somewhere, "Eye has not seen, nor ear heard, nor have entered into the heart of man the things which God has prepared for those who love Him."[4])

Watch God's plan in action—humiliation and elevation are about to switch places.

"Excellent!" the king said to Haman. "Hurry and get the robe and my horse, and do just as you have said for Mordecai the Jew,

who sits at the gate of the palace. Do not fail to carry out everything *you* have suggested." *So Haman took the robe and put it on
Mordecai, placed him on the king's own horse, and led him through
the city square, shouting, "This is what happens to those the king
wishes to honor!"* Afterward Mordecai returned to the palace gate,
but Haman hurried home dejected and completely *humiliated*
["with his head covered"—NIV, NKJV)].[5]

With one command, a sleep-deprived king shattered Haman's lifelong
dream and elevated a prejudged man to the height of power in the empire.
Xerxes unknowingly commanded Mordecai's bitterest enemy to honor him
as if he were the king of Persia; and he humiliated the man who was once
the empire's most feared politician and enforcer. You can blame it on the
queen's rich homemade dessert, or you can credit the God who guided
Esther's shrewd strategy.

Haman's bad day was about to get even worse, and Esther's good day
just got better! I feel the same way about the days in which we live. Satan
is about to have a bad day, and the bride is about to experience a good one!
It is all about finding favor with the King and preparing for your moment
in His presence.

Haman hurries home with a covered head, hoping to find solace in the
"ever-supportive" words of his wife.

> When Haman told his wife, Zeresh, and all his friends what
> had happened, they said, "Since Mordecai—this man who has
> humiliated you—is a Jew, *you will never succeed in your plans
> against him. It will be fatal to continue to oppose him.*" While
> they were still talking, the king's eunuchs arrived to take Haman
> to the banquet Esther had prepared.[6]

Note that the Scripture says *"never succeed."* If you are a child of God,
take this promise to heart: "No weapon formed against you shall prosper,
and every tongue which rises against you in judgment you shall con-
demn."[7]

This leads us to what may be one of the greatest of all the lessons in
Esther's life: *Refine your pursuit to the point where you genuinely value the*

King more than the kingdom; you'll be amazed to discover what the King will do for you.

Esther had a desperate need. Her future was at stake and that of her people—they were to be killed; they were going to be slaughtered. But she had to set aside her fear and prepare for her moment. It took three visits before she sensed it was time to appeal to the king's heart.

THE KING'S HEART IS SOFT TOWARD YOU

The King's heart is soft toward you, but you must set aside your need for just a moment. The protocol of the King's presence teaches us to honor Him before we ask Him! Don't talk to God about your need; instead, pour your love upon Him until you get to the place of worship and intimacy.

PROTOCOL *of the* PALACE

9. The deeper you go into the palace, the fewer the people, but the greater the provision!

I'm acting as the King's chamberlain right now. You are a potential Esther.

Red is His favorite color; clothe yourself in the blood of Calvary.

Put on the garments of praise—put them on and exchange worship for heaviness, no matter how you feel. Soak in the anointing oil.

If you can forget about your needs long enough to serve at the table of God and minister to His hunger with your worship . . . then the heavens may literally be the limit to what He will do for you and give to you. There is an amazing axiom: *"The deeper you go into the palace, the fewer the people, but the greater the provision!"*

Not many will learn the lessons necessary to gain their access to the inner recesses of the palace. It takes too much time, requires too much preparation, and forces them to subrogate their ego to the King's desires.

Not everyone is willing to do that. I can't do it for you—no one can. I'm just a chamberlain.

I can't make anything happen, but I can pray that you learn the lessons necessary to pass through the outer courts and into the place of intimate worship.

For those who *will* listen and learn: *The deeper you go into the palace, the fewer the people, but the greater the provision!*

CHAPTER 12

HAPPILY EVER AFTER

*Living in the King's House
and Wearing the King's Ring*

The early-morning light brought dramatic changes to the city of Susa. It also signaled a 180-degree change in the direction of the winds of destiny. What a difference a day makes—twenty-four short hours! Some days seem more important than others, and some victories more significant than others.

The day Haman and King Xerxes sat down at Queen Esther's second banquet marked one of the greatest victories in the memory of the Jewish people. The events of this day (and the night before it) would lead to one of the most momentous turnarounds in human history.

It came about through the invisible hand of God—a God who is mentioned in the book of Esther only in a hidden acrostic allegedly repeated several times in the original Hebrew manuscripts.[1] (Out of sight does not mean out of play! God was still in the game.) The hidden workings of an all-powerful God saved the day. It would be a day of *demonic demotion* and *heavenly promotion* in the sight of an entire nation. A divine reversal!

Remember the ancient Hebrew promise echoed in the Scriptures: *Men may throw the dice, but it is God who determines where they fall.*[2] This was not to be a day of mourning but a day of joyous celebration for God's people.

On the night before, the king had paced restlessly through his royal residence, and finally he called for his best sleeping aid, the royal records. Haman had returned home from Queen Esther's first banquet to rehearse his glories to family and friends and to bitterly plot his revenge on Mordecai the Jew that very same night.

As for Queen Esther, perhaps she had made her early preparations for the king and then went to sleep. Because we aren't told otherwise, Mordecai presumably remained in sackcloth and ashes outside the king's gate or went home to await another day in the ashes of impending doom.

HAMAN'S DECREE AUTHORIZED THE MURDER OF EVERY JEW

As "that day" dawned, Haman's decree, sealed with the signet ring of Xerxes, had been delivered to all 127 provinces stretching from India to Ethiopia. It specifically authorized the murder of every Jew in the Persian empire; it also authorized the subsequent plundering of the Jews' wealth to finance the ethnic cleansing.

The enemies of the Jews were making their weapons ready, and anticipation was high in Haman's camp. Everyone who had ever been offended by them, or become jealous of the Jews, eagerly looked forward to the day when they could "legally" eradicate the Jewish foreigners and plunder their goods. (Meanwhile, the friends of the Jews shook their heads and wondered at this strange turn of events.)

The city of Susa was confused. Genocide seemed imminent and irreversible. The earthly law of the Medes and Persians, once given, could not be rescinded.

Despite all of the risks, labor, and preparation Esther had made, she seemed to be no closer to winning an executive pardon for the Jews than she was the day before. Only one more banquet remained, and she knew she couldn't stall the king much longer. Maybe she rose with the sun to busy herself with preparations. Choosing to focus on the king, she remained seemingly oblivious to what was happening outside the walls of the royal palace.

Have you found yourself weary, discouraged, and seemingly no farther down the road of life than when you first entered the valley of trial and tribulation? Did you quit, or did you begin walking again, step by step? Have you *ever* lived, like the people of Susa, in confusing times or circumstances?

How many dawns must we see before we believe that the sun's faithful rising and setting simply reflect the faithfulness of the invisible God, the One who put the planets into orbit and who maintains the orbital spin of our own lives in grace?

Imagine the shock that hit the residents of a city satiated with the pomp and circumstance of royal comings and goings. They had seen many things pass by their shops, homes, and markets, but this was a sight that astounded them.

> PROTOCOL *of the* PALACE
> 10. When your enemy plots your demise, your King is planning your reward.

The great Haman, the feared vizier and powerful prime minister of the Persian empire, was circumnavigating the city streets while leading around Mordecai the Jew, mounted on the king's own horse!

Mordecai was receiving his own private parade! Haman is in the humiliating posture of being a servant to the man for whom he built a gallows the previous night! What a life lesson! *The same night your enemy is plotting your demise, your King is planning your reward.*

Haman learned the unpleasant corollary to that divine law: The same night you are planning your proud reward, God may be orchestrating your humiliating fall. The Scriptures warn the proud: "Pride goes before destruction, and a haughty spirit before a fall."[3]

Satan may have plans for you, but so does God! "For I know the thoughts that I think toward you, says the LORD, thoughts of peace and not of evil, to give you a future and a hope."[4]

Observe God's plans for Mordecai!

Haman, the man in command who was second only to the great King Xerxes, had arrayed Mordecai in the king's robes and mounted him on the king's stallion bearing the king's royal insignia. Under normal circumstances, these were considered capital offenses worthy of the most painful death. Most amazing of all, Haman himself, nervously glancing from side to side as if in mortal fear, was shouting the praises of Mordecai the Jew in the city square: *"This is what happens to those the king wishes to honor!"*[5]

Some rabbinic sources teach that Haman had to act as Mordecai's "personal servant" by personally washing and dressing this man who had spent several days of mourning on an ash pile. They also say Haman had to "lower himself so that Mordecai could step upon his neck in order to mount the horse, since Mordecai was so weak from fasting."[6]

To make things worse, according to the rabbis, Haman's daughter thought the man on the king's horse was Haman and that the man leading the horse was Mordecai. Eager to humiliate her father's worst enemy, she leaned over the edge of her roof and emptied an overfull chamber pot (perhaps we should simply call it a portable toilet) onto the head of the man she thought was the despised Jew.

When the foul contents hit the mark, the victim looked up, and the daughter realized she had just humiliated her own father! The rabbis say she immediately fell off the roof and died.[7]

> Afterward Mordecai returned to the palace gate, but *Haman hurried home dejected and completely humiliated.* When Haman told his wife, Zeresh, and all his friends what had happened, they said, "Since Mordecai—this man who has humiliated you—is a Jew, you will never succeed in your plans against him. It will be fatal to continue to oppose him." While they were still talking, the king's eunuchs arrived to take Haman to the banquet Esther had prepared.[8]

Haman's misery and humiliation in the moments before the king's eunuchs arrived was far worse than any of us can imagine. Things were about to go from bad to worse for Haman, the enemy of the Jews. Perhaps he hardly had time to wash off the stench before he was hustled to the banquet—the second banquet.

The utterly complete reversal of his fortune, by God's divine decree, was at hand. The scriptural narrative is powerful in its simplicity:

> So the king and Haman went to Queen Esther's banquet. And while they were drinking wine that day, the king again asked her, "Tell me what you want, Queen Esther. What is your request? I will give it to you, even if it is half the kingdom!"
>
> And so Queen Esther replied, "If Your Majesty is pleased with me and wants to grant my request, my petition is that my life and the lives of my people will be spared. For my people and I have been sold to those who would kill, slaughter, and annihilate us. If we had only been sold as slaves, I could remain quiet, for that

would have been a matter too trivial to warrant disturbing the king."

"Who would do such a thing?" King Xerxes demanded. "Who would dare touch you?"

Esther replied, *"This wicked Haman is our enemy."* Haman grew pale with fright before the king and queen.[9]

When it turns, *it turns*! Watch the timing of this divine reversal. We are seconds into a few destiny-altering moments. The preparation process was long—but the moment of favor came quickly.

Favor makes you fearful to your enemies.

If it is true that with the Lord a day is as a thousand years, then perhaps it might be said that divine favor will restore in a day what was stolen over a lifetime.

THE PLOT OF THE ENEMY BECOMES THE OPPORTUNITY OF GOD

Esther's story is a dramatic chronicle of a series of divine reversals:

A peasant becomes a princess and is crowned queen.
The plot of the enemy becomes the opportunity of God.
Mordecai receives a heavenly promotion and is delivered *from* death.
Haman is subjected to a demonic demotion and delivered *to* death.

God is *looking* for a chance to humiliate the enemy of your destiny. Before it's all over, even Satan will be confessing that Jesus Christ is Lord!

Note how Esther sets this up.

The queen uses her learned skills to enhance her ability to communicate vividly to the king. She uses three specific words, registering ever-progressive levels of violence and mayhem, to describe her danger, saying she had been sold to those who would *kill, slaughter,* and *annihilate* them. (I wonder if she was thinking the men would be killed, the women slaughtered, and the children—and the future of the Jewish race—annihilated?)

The description sounds extremely familiar to the description Jesus gave for the great thief of the world: "The thief's purpose is to steal and kill and destroy." (To steal your strength, kill your present, and destroy your future—that is what Satan has planned. Now read the rest of the verse to hear what God has planned for you.) "My purpose is to give life in all its fullness."[10]

Whatever Esther was thinking, we know her words hit the king's heart like fiery darts. This supreme earthly monarch had already demonstrated the lethal force of his royal rage, but it seems that nothing had enraged him to this level before.

HAMAN HAD A "FEARFUL EXPECTATION OF JUDGMENT"

I read something in the book of Hebrews that must come close to describing the terror Haman felt that day as Queen Esther's final words echoed in the stunned silence. As the king's wine goblet hung suspended midway between the magnificent banqueting table and his own lips, Haman must have felt a heart-stopping dread, "a certain fearful expectation of judgment, and fiery indignation which will devour the adversaries."[11]

Perhaps we are now just under a minute into the turnaround!

> Then the king jumped to his feet in a rage and went out into the palace garden. But Haman stayed behind to plead for his life with Queen Esther, for he knew that he was doomed. In despair he fell on the couch where Queen Esther was reclining, just as the king returned from the palace garden. "Will he even assault the queen right here in the palace, before my very eyes?" the king roared. And as soon as the king spoke, his attendants covered Haman's face, signaling his doom.[12]

With the sudden covering of Haman's face, his descent into doom was seemingly complete. This was reserved only for the shameful, the bitter of heart, and those condemned to death.

Only that morning Haman had cheerfully dressed in his best, hoping to see the elaborate plans of sweet revenge he had crafted in the previous night hours finally carried out against Mordecai the Jew.

He walked out of his expansive residence and lingered in the shadow of the seventy-five-foot pole erected in his courtyard. He was particularly proud of the sharpened point at the top—a perfect instrument of death by impalement.

That is what gallows were to ancient Persians. Yes, people were hung from the gallows, but not by a noose around the neck. They were impaled on the sharp point and hung there, suspended in the air, until they died.

Within moments of entering the royal courts where Haman had formerly wielded such unprecedented power, the king ordered him to honor his hated enemy with every elaborate honor Haman had secretly desired (and then prescribed) for himself.

CAUGHT AND IMPALED ON HIS OWN TOWER OF PROUD WORDS

Now Haman had been caught and impaled on his own tower of proud words. In a matter of seconds his destiny had been reduced to a brief and violent litany of destruction. With nowhere else to turn, the fallen schemer decided on impulse that he would beg the queen for mercy while the king looked for the armed guards who had been dismissed for the intimate banquet with Esther.

How long can it take for a king to summon his bodyguards? (Perhaps it took no more than a couple of minutes.)

We don't know whether Haman "slipped" or simply "sprawled" across Queen Esther's lap in paralyzing fear, but there can be no mistake about how the king viewed his actions. One of the king's chamberlains quickly volunteered some information that put the final nail in Haman's coffin of secret plots and premeditated murder. (Perhaps we are at three minutes now!)

> Then Harbona, one of the king's eunuchs, said, "Haman has set up a gallows that stands seventy-five feet tall in his own courtyard. He intended to use it to hang Mordecai, the man who saved the king from assassination."
> "Then hang Haman on it!" the king ordered.[13]

It probably took less than five minutes for Haman to plummet from privilege at a worshiping banquet to destruction as a vanquished enemy!

So they hanged Haman on the gallows he had set up for Mordecai, and the king's anger was pacified. On that same day King Xerxes gave the estate of Haman, the enemy of the Jews, to Queen Esther. Then Mordecai was brought before the king, for Esther had told the king how they were related. The king took off his signet ring—which he had taken back from Haman—and gave it to Mordecai. And Esther appointed Mordecai to be in charge of Haman's property.[14]

A PUBLIC DISPLAY OF HAMAN'S HUMILIATION

I've heard it said that Haman's seventy-five-foot stake was a monument to the excess of his prideful ego. Whatever else it was, it became the instrument of his death and a public display of his utter humiliation.

I know of Another who, in His humble obedience, "disarmed principalities and powers [and] made a public spectacle of them, triumphing over them" using His own body nailed to a bloody stake on a hill called Calvary.[15]

(The sudden and sure judgment of King Xerxes reminds me of the certain judgment pronounced by the greater and higher King of Kings over the father of all liars, the archplotter against the kingdom of God.[16])

It was common in ancient kingdoms for the property of convicted criminals to revert back to the crown.[17] The confiscation of Haman's properties and power reminds me of the heavenly monarch who "led captivity captive, and gave gifts to men."[18] In both cases, *the plunder of hell was used to provide for heaven's children.*

I also read somewhere that "a good man leaves an inheritance to his children's children, but the wealth of the sinner is stored up for the righteous."[19] This is yet another grand reversal influenced and empowered by our invisible King on behalf of those in His favor.

What a difference a day makes! Because Esther found favor with the king, in three days she passed from probable death in the throne room to a fairy-tale existence "living happily ever after" in the house and intimate favor of the king.

FAVOR ELEVATED MORDECAI FROM CLERK TO PRIME MINISTER

> PROTOCOL *of the* PALACE
>
> 11. Favor can restore in a day what was stolen over a lifetime.

In one day favor transported Mordecai from mourning on a pile of ashes, wearing sackcloth outside the king's gate, to being celebrated while wearing the king's robes and riding the king's warhorse through the city! We know that with the Lord a day is as a thousand years; then perhaps it might be said that God can pack a thousand years' worth of favor into a single day. Favor can restore in a day what was stolen over a lifetime. Ultimately, favor elevated him from a clerk's table at the outer door of the palace to the office of prime minister at the king's side in the royal court. Imagine his wearing the king's ring and exercising the authority of the king himself.

There will come a day when the robes of the King's righteousness are placed around the shoulders of faithful worshipers and they sit astride one of the King's horses to be paraded into a celestial battleground to see the glory of the King revealed in battle.[20]

Esther's obedience, courage, and understanding of the protocol of the king's presence had brought salvation to her and promotion to Mordecai.

But something was *still* wrong.

THE VIRUS OF ETHNIC CLEANSING OPERATES ON AUTOMATIC PILOT

The decree of death against the Jews was still in effect in every province of Persia. A lethal anti-Semitic virus had been planted in the empire that operated on auto-pilot. It would annihilate the Jews even though its engineer and creator was dead! Once again, Esther approached the king's throne unannounced.

> Now once more Esther came before the king, falling down at his feet and begging him with tears to stop Haman's evil plot against the Jews. Again the king held out the gold scepter to Esther. So she rose and stood before him and said, "If Your Majesty is pleased with me and if he thinks it is right, send out a decree reversing Haman's orders to destroy the Jews throughout all the provinces of the king. For how can I endure to see my people and my family slaughtered and destroyed?"[21]

Esther's desperate prayer echoes the countless prayers we send heavenward every day. We beg God to defeat our enemies and reenact a battle that was won two thousand years ago. In much the same way that King Xerxes responded to Esther,[22] our King has gently reminded us that He already placed His signet ring on our finger when He gave us the power and right to use His name in the earth.

It is up to *us* to send the message in the King's name. I seem to remember His saying, "I will give you the keys of the kingdom of heaven, and whatever you bind on earth will be bound in heaven, and whatever you loose on earth will be loosed in heaven."[23]

VICTORY SHOULD BE HAPPENING IN THE HEAVENLIES AT THIS MOMENT

What happened in Esther's day is a natural picture of a supernatural truth that *should* be happening in the heavenlies this very moment as we praise and worship our King.

> So on March 7 the two decrees of the king were put into effect. On that day, the enemies of the Jews had hoped to destroy them, *but quite the opposite happened.* The Jews gathered in their cities throughout all the king's provinces *to defend themselves against anyone who might try to harm them.* But no one could make a stand against them, for everyone was afraid of them.[24]

And all the commanders of the provinces, the princes, the governors, and the royal officials helped the Jews for fear of Mordecai. . . .

> Favor makes you fearful to your enemies.

The Jews went ahead on the appointed day and struck down their enemies with the sword. They killed and annihilated their enemies and did as they pleased with those who hated them.[25]

The modern "sensibilities" of some Christians in what we call more civilized times are offended by any mention of military conflict, combat, or death in time of war. Some are thoroughly convinced that war is never justified, and it is their right to hold that opinion.

However, we are commanded to *hate sin* in God's Word. Whether we glean spiritual insight from the natural battles or the spiritual truths in Esther, it is clear that God wants to eradicate every form and shadow of sin so He can fellowship freely with His creation. That is why He gave His Son as a sacrifice on the cross.

Haman, an Amalekite and direct descendant of King Agag from Saul's day, represents sin in all of its malignant evil and hatred of what is good. The Bible says the Jews defended themselves when they were attacked and that they killed five hundred enemies in Susa alone. You must have a killer instinct when it comes to sin. It might be hard to picture elegant Esther in that light . . . until you realize what she was fighting for! You also are fighting for your family, your friends, and your nation! To what extent will you go in order to complete the victory?

The ten sons of Haman were also killed, but there were still armed enemies threatening the Jews in that city. It is at this point that King Xerxes asked what more he could do for Queen Esther, and she made an odd request (in the opinion of certain critics):

[King Xerxes] called for Queen Esther and said, "The Jews have killed five hundred people in the fortress of Susa alone and also Haman's ten sons. If they have done that here, what has happened in the rest of the provinces? But now, what more do you want? It will be granted to you; tell me and I will do it." And Esther said, "If it please Your Majesty, give the Jews in Susa permission *to do again tomorrow as they have done today,* and have the bodies of Haman's ten sons hung from the gallows."[26]

When the King asks, "What more do you want?"—always reply, "Complete victory!"

This is yet another valuable lesson from Esther: *God will give you an extra day to make sure your victory is complete!* He said, "I will give you back what you lost to the stripping locusts."[27]

Wasn't it crass of Esther to ask the king, "Give us another day to kill our enemies"? In our day, this is called "running up the score." Sometimes, in sports, well-meaning coaches who perhaps don't have the killer instinct will say, "I don't want to run up the score." It may surprise you to know there is evidence in the Scriptures that God at times gives us extra innings just to run up the score on evil!

> God will give you an extra day to make sure your victory is complete!

ELEVATION — HUMILIATION

Esther's life teaches us: *The wisdom of the King will use the same process that elevates you to humiliate the enemy.*

The same water in the Red Sea that provided a route of escape for the children of Israel also proved to be a grave for the enemy that pursued them.

It may feel as if the enemy is close on your heels, but by the time the King is finished with him, even Lucifer will bow down and call Him Lord![28]

Contrary to popular opinion, *hate is a necessary part of the Christian vocabulary.* We are commanded by God to love righteousness and *hate* sin.[29]

As beautiful as Esther was, hidden deep within her was a steely resolve *to finish what Saul had left undone.* Although this warrior-king stood head and shoulders above his countrymen, he did not have what it took to obey God and utterly destroy the Amalekites. He was strong in body but soft in character. Esther may have been soft in body, but she was strong in character.

A killer instinct rose up in Queen Esther, and she said to herself, "Not only am I going to make sure *we* survive, but I'm going to make sure *he doesn't.*" She was determined to fulfill God's mandate: *Haman, the last of the murderous line of King Agag the Amalekite, must not survive.* (Nor would *any offspring* of his spirit.)

Could this be yet another embodiment of the prophetic words God spoke to Satan the serpent? "And I will put enmity between you and the woman, and between your offspring and hers; he will crush your head, and you will strike his heel."[30]

> So the king agreed, and the decree was announced in Susa. They also hung the bodies of Haman's ten sons from the gallows. Then the Jews at Susa gathered together on March 8 and killed three hundred more people, though again they took no plunder. Meanwhile, the other Jews throughout the king's provinces had *gathered together to defend their lives. They gained relief from all their enemies,* killing seventy-five thousand of those who hated them. But they did not take any plunder.[31]

Esther was not and *could not* be content merely to see Haman eliminated. We must remember what we learned earlier: *What you do not eradicate when you are strong will come back to attack you when you are weak.*

Haman had planted a lethal virus of hatred and genocide throughout the Persian empire. A man of hate had engineered the destruction of the Jews without knowledge or input. If they did not act, they would be destroyed even after the "father" of the plot was dead.

Esther set out to *put her heel on the head of illegitimate authority.* I am convinced that, at times, lethal force must be met by lethal force. As for the Jews, it seems clear that they acted primarily in self-defense, and they waged war only against those who attacked them with malice and weapons of destruction. They even refused to follow the cultural norm and plunder the goods of their enemies.

Why were the bodies of Haman's ten sons hung from the gallows? It was the cultural wartime equivalent of cutting the basketball nets off the goals, of waving the grudge trophy in front of the television cameras, and of publicly pulling down the statues of evil tyrants.

YOU STARTED IT, NOW WE WILL *FINISH* IT

Esther was making a clear statement to the enemies of the Jewish people: "You started it without cause. Now this is going to be such a lopsided victory that we will never have to fight this battle again." Once their enemies started the fight, the Jews saw to it that they *finished it.*

Is God really in favor of running up the score like this? Well, one time He stopped the sun to make sure that His people had enough daylight left to complete their victory.[32] This gives us a whole new slant on the biblical maxim, "Do not let the sun go down on your wrath."[33] Finish the fight!

It is up to us in our day to bring closure and to destroy the lingering works of the enemy. Adopt Esther's tactics. We must use the "signet ring" of the King's name while wearing the garments of praise, worship, and righteousness. We win spiritual battles by taking up the weapons of our warfare through passionate praise and indulgent worship.

> The bride has no worries when the enemy has no sons.

Isn't that a little too warlike for loving Christians? I remember someone in the Bible who said something to the church that is also very warlike:

> For the *weapons of our warfare* are not carnal but *mighty in God*
> for pulling down strongholds, casting down arguments and every
> high thing that exalts itself against the knowledge of God, bringing

every thought into captivity to the obedience of Christ, and being ready *to punish all disobedience* when your obedience is fulfilled.[34]

How do we reconcile the peasant who became a princess bride with the queen who waged war at the end of the book of Esther? As long as you tolerate sin within the palace, it multiplies. You must eradicate the enemy in your day of strength. *The bride has no worries when the enemy has no sons.* The line of the Agagites was gone; joy had come in the morning.

> Finish the fight, and future generations can celebrate!

Esther's story is the ultimate journal of divine reversal. Mordecai, ever the scribe, chronicled the aftermath when he wrote a letter to the Jews throughout the Persian empire.

He told them to *celebrate* these days with feasting and gladness and by giving gifts to each other and to the poor. This would commemorate a time when the Jews gained relief from their enemies, when their sorrow was turned into gladness and their mourning into joy.[35]

This two-day celebration came to be known as Purim, because Haman originally set the date of the Jews' demise by casting *pur* (or dice). How would you like to have a day named for your victory? A day *named* for your enemy but *celebrated* by you! Never underestimate how a *bad* day can be transformed into a *good* day by worship!

This celebration is still held today in Israel and among Jewish communities around the world. *Finish the fight, and future generations can celebrate!*

WHAT HAMAN MEANT FOR DESTRUCTION, GOD MEANT FOR LIBERATION

I can almost hear Mordecai, the prime minister, telling his fellow Jews in his letter, "Long before Haman cast the dice (*pur*) to set the day of our destruction, this day had been set by the Almighty for our liberation. This day was decreed and destined to be a day of celebration and not of mourning. So from this time forward, we are going to celebrate this day!"

Purim pictures both the divine deliverance of the Jews from a genocidal plot and the intimate love of a God Chaser for the presence of the King of Kings. This holiday of delight, triumph, and thanksgiving celebrates our divine deliverance from a decree of death.

It is the festival of Psalm 23, when we sing to the Lord, "*You prepare a feast for me in the presence of my enemies. You welcome me as a guest, anointing my head with oil. My cup overflows with blessings.*"[36]

When we worship Him, the King moves heaven and earth to reverse the judgments, plots, and schemes against us, resulting in our heavenly promotion, while bringing down our true enemy (Satan) in demonic demotion. Amazingly, the Scriptures end with the Bride being caught *up*, while Satan is cast *down*!

Simple decisions made by a powerful king altered a people's destiny! But those decisions were influenced by a young Jewish girl named Esther. Pulled from her comfort zone and thrust into a plush but dangerous environment, she waged a wise war of worship, ultimately "*finding favor with the king!*"

You, too, can find favor with the King—preparing for your moment in His presence.

PROTOCOL *of the* PALACE

12. One night with the King changes everything!

From the first blushing glance of a young girl toward her beloved, to the passionate pursuit of a bride and groom—love is indivisible from life. The greatest lesson we may learn from Esther is simply, *Fall in love with the King!*

Discover the wonder of the King's presence. You've been chosen for such a time as this! You too are destined for the palace, the place of His presence. *Prepare for your moment in His presence. Prepare for your moment of divine favor!*

Learn the protocol of His presence; learn how to shed your peasant ways and carry yourself like a princess. Wear His favorite color. Decide you will no longer shout your demands from the gates.

Once you've learned the protocol of His presence, once you've mastered the art of preparation, you can whisper your wishes from the intimate embrace of worship instead of announcing your requests in formal petition from the outer courts.

When the church, the bride of the King, whispers her heart's desire, her King's heart is moved, and kingdoms begin to shift like pawns on a chessboard.

Why worry and fret over your fate? Prepare for your moment of favor! Intimacy with the King holds the key to your future!

Esther had a blind date with her destiny, and so can you. *Never underestimate the potential of **one** worship encounter.*

It only takes one night with the King to turn a peasant into a princess! One moment of favor can change everything. Thirty seconds in His presence can change your destiny!

Never underestimate the potential of one encounter. One moment of favor with a sovereign monarch can forever change your course.

One night with the King changes everything!

I would love to hear from you. There are many more Esther resources available online, including an audio version of this book. Please visit **www.godchasers.net** and share your thoughts and ideas with **me**.

Tony Tony

Twelve Protocols of the Palace

Esther's Secrets of Finding Favor With the King

1. Never underestimate the potential of one encounter.

2. Seek the heart of the King, not the splendor of His kingdom.

3. One day of favor can be worth more than a lifetime of labor.

4. Worship is the protocol that protects the King and qualifies the visitor.

5. Influence flows from intimacy, and access comes from relationship.

6. If you learn what the King favors, you can become a favorite.

7. If your enemy is the King's enemy, then your battle is the King's battle.

8. Favor is what happens when preparation meets opportunity.

9. The deeper you go into the palace, the fewer the people, but the greater the provision.

10. When your enemy plots your demise, your King is planning your reward.

11. Favor can restore in a day what was stolen over a lifetime.

12. One night with the King changes everything!

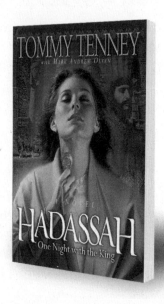

TOMMY TENNEY is the author of the multimillion-selling THE GOD CHASERS series, including *God's Favorite House, The God Catchers, God's Eye View,* and *The Prayers of a God Chaser.* Adding to that series are, *How to Be a God Chaser and a Kid Chaser,* coauthored with his mother, and *Chasing God, Serving Man,* a revelatory revisiting of the story of Mary and Martha. He is also the author of another series of books on unity, including *God's Dream Team, Answering God's Prayer,* and *God's Secret to Greatness.* Coauthoring other books such as *Secret Sources of Power* and *On Daddy's Shoulders* has helped him fulfill his mandate to spread the gospel through writing.

Tommy is a prolific author with more than one million books in print each year and eight bestselling titles to date. His books have been translated into more than 30 languages and have been nominated for many awards, including the Gold Medallion Award and Retailers' Book of the Year.

Tommy spent 10 years pastoring and has spent over 20 years in itinerant ministry, traveling to more than 40 nations. He speaks in over 150 venues each year, sharing his heart with many thousands. The GodChasers television ministry is seen in over 120 nations on many different networks. His ministry Web site, *www.godchasers.net,* is viewed on average by more than one million people per month.

Tommy is passionate about the presence of God and unity in the body. To help others pursue these twin passions, he founded *GodChasers.network,* a mission ministry organized to assist pastors globally and to distribute Tommy's teachings through various media.

Three generations of ministry in his family heritage have given Tommy a rich perspective. He has a gifting to lead hungry people into the presence of God. He and his wife, Jeannie, understand the value of intimacy with God and humility in serving God's people.

The Tenneys reside in Louisiana with their three daughters and two Yorkies.

Endnotes

Chapter 1

1. Internet source: *www.royalty.nu/Europe/England/Windsor/Diana.html*. Accessed 24 February 03.
2. Esther 1:10–12, emphasis mine.
3. See Esther 1:19.
4. Esther 7:8 NLT, emphasis mine.
5. See, for example, Ephesians 5:25–27.
6. Perhaps a measure of Esther's importance is the degree of resistance to its message. It is one of the most misunderstood and neglected books of the Bible! It has been hated by the late and the great of human history and the church. Even Martin Luther, the celebrated Protestant church reformer, did his best to have Esther removed from the Protestant canon (the officially accepted and approved books of the Bible). According to Dr. Karen H. Jobes, a noted Bible scholar, in *The NIV Application Commentary: Esther* (Grand Rapids, Mich.: Zondervan, 1999), 21: "Martin Luther denounced this book together with the apocryphal 2 Maccabees, saying of them, 'I am so great an enemy to the second book of Maccabees, and to Esther, that I wish they had not come to us at all, for they have too many heathen unnaturalities'" [citing Martin Luther, *The Table Talk of Martin Luther,* William Hazlitt, trans. (Philadelphia: United Lutheran Publication House, n.d.), 13.].
7. Jobes, 45; citing Robert Gordis, *Megillat Esther* (New York: Ktav, 1974), 13–14, emphasis mine.
8. Joyce G. Baldwin, *Esther: An Introduction & Commentary* [Tyndale Old Testament Commentaries, D. J. Wiseman, gen. ed.] (Downers Grove, Ill.: InterVarsity Press, 1984), 66. The author writes: "According to Josephus there were four hundred, but Paton, estimating at the rate of a different girl per night for four years (16; cf. 1:3), arrives at 1,460."
9. Jobes, 96, citing Megillah 15a (the scroll of Esther).
10. Ibid., 94, citing Loeb Classical Library: Herodotus, 3.8.
11. Ibid., citing Plutarch, who reported "that other Persian kings did sometimes marry, contrary to law, women with whom they had fallen passionately in love" (Loeb Classical Library: *Plutarch's Lives,* Artazerxes 23.3).
12. See Esther 2:12.
13. See Matthew 1:5–6. Both of these couples were ancestors of David, who was a

natural ancestor of Joseph and a spiritual type and shadow of Jesus Christ, "the son of David."

14. Jobes, 61, citing Herodotus 17.66.

15. Esther 2:2–4, emphasis mine.

16. Esther 2:12, emphasis mine.

17. Ecclesiastes 10:1a KJV.

18. Beelzebub is common terminology for Lucifer. The literal translation is "lord of the flies, or god of dung" (*Strong's Greek Concordance*, 954).

19. Jobes points out that spices and fragrant oils were a major Persian export, and she cites the findings of a world-renowned archeologist to illustrate the way spices were probably used to prepare Esther for her fateful night with the king: "W. F. Albright has argued that cube-shaped spice burners excavated at the ancient site of Lachish in Israel were not for burning incense at religious rituals, as originally thought, but were cosmetic burners used by women to prepare their skin and clothing with the scent of oil of roses, oil of cloves, and essence of musk (scents still popular among perfumers today). Albright proposes that such cosmetic devices were used by women widely throughout the ancient world for both hygienic and therapeutic value. The fragrant oil would be placed in the cosmetic burner and heated in a fire. The woman would perfume her skin and clothing by crouching naked over the burner with her robe draped over her body like a tent. Albright cites this passage from Esther as a biblical example of this process" (p. 110, citing William Foxwell Albright, "The Lachish Cosmetic Burner and Esther 2:12," reprinted in *Studies in the Book of Esther*, Carey A. Moore, ed. [New York: Ktav, 1982], 361–68).

20. See Matthew 2:1–11.

21. See Luke 7:36–37.

22. See Matthew 26:6–13. (Mark 14:3 records the same incident but calls the mixture "spikenard" or "pure oil of nard," which was an aromatic of some kind.)

23. See Mark 15:23, 34.

24. See John 19:39.

25. Evidently there is more power in myrrh than anyone but God realized. Researchers at Rutgers University discovered that myrrh contains "furanosesquiterpenoid," a compound that is very toxic to cancer cells. It appears to deactivate a protein in cancer cells that resists chemotherapy. In lab studies, it was effective against leukemia and cancer of the breast, prostate, ovary, and lung! ("Discovery Finds Myrrh Kills Cancer," Gannett News Service, appearing in *The Des Moines Register*, Monday, Dec. 17, 2001.)

Chapter 2

1. Definition for "porphyry" from the *Holman Bible Dictionary* (Nashville: Holman Bible Publishers, 1991). Accessed via The QuickVerse Library software, by Parsons Technology, Inc., One Parsons Drive, PO Box 100, Hiawatha, IA 52233–0100.

2. Esther 1:6–7 NLT, emphasis mine.

3. See Proverbs 18:16.

4. See 1 Kings 11:1–3.

5. See Acts 10:34 and John 4:23–24 NLT, respectively.

6. John 3:16 NLT, emphasis mine.

7. Isaiah 45:15 NLT, emphasis mine.

8. 2 Timothy 2:15 NASB.

9. Jobes, 21: "In Hebrew narrative, character is often revealed only through action and

speech, leaving the reader to draw inferences about motives and intentions. True to Hebrew narrative style, in the book of Esther the outward, observable events are stated without explanation or comment."

10. Ibid., 28, summarized from Herodotus's descriptions and writings in Loeb Classical Library, A. D. Godley, trans. (New York: G. P. Putnam's Sons, 1922).

11. Charles R. Swindoll, *Esther: A Woman of Strength and Dignity* (Nashville: Word, 1997), 43–44.

12. Ibid., 45.

13. It sounds strange to hear the Persian King Darius called a "chosen vessel of God," but it is true. In fact, God used three members of the Achaemenid family line to accomplish His will. Cyrus the Great fulfilled Bible prophecy when he conquered the Babylonian empire that had captured Jerusalem and destroyed the temple (see 2 Chronicles 36:22–23; Ezra 1:1–4; Isaiah 44:28–45:15). Xerxes' father, Darius, actually funded the cost to rebuild the temple in Jerusalem and cooperated with Zerubbabel and the high priest, Jeshua (Ezra 6:8–9). Xerxes was instrumental in preserving and elevating the Jewish people, through Esther's intervention, in the book of Esther.

Chapter 3

1. *Merriam-Webster's Collegiate Dictionary, Tenth Edition* (Springfield, Mass.: Merriam-Webster, Incorporated, 1994), 939.

2. Isaiah 14:13.

3. Mark 6:4b NIV.

4. A. S. Van Der Woude, gen. ed., *The World of the Bible: Bible Handbook, Volume 1* (Grand Rapids, Mich.: Eerdmans, 1986), 321. The editors note that King Xerxes was ultimately assassinated in his own bedchambers by Artabanus, in 465 B.C., and succeeded by his son, Artaxerxes I.

5. Latin for "unacceptable person."

6. "Aristotle on Persian Court Life," an article based on a translation of Aristotle's "On the Cosmos, to Alexander" (398a11–398b1), D. J. Furley, trans. Drawn from Giovanni Reale and Abraham P. Bos, *Il trattato "Sul cosmo per Alessandro" attribuito ad Aristotele. Monografia introduttiva, testo greco con traduzione a fronte, commentario, bibliografia ragionata e indici* (Milan, 1995). Accessed via the Internet at *www.livius.org/aj-al/alexander/alexander_t38.html* on 4 March 2003.

7. A stade was a Greek measure of distance ranging from 607 to 738 feet, according to *Merriam-Webster's Collegiate Dictionary,* 1143, definitions for "stade" and "stadium."

8. J. M. Cook, *The Persian Empire* (London: J. M. Dent & Sons Ltd., 1983), 143. The author says this official was possibly called the *azarapates* or referred to by the Old Persian term *hazarapatish* ("commander of a thousand"). The Greek historians referred to this officer using a Greek term, *chiliarch,* with the same meaning.

9. Adapted from Ephesians 4:21–24 NLT: "Since you have heard all about him and have learned the truth that is in Jesus, throw off your old evil nature and your former way of life, which is rotten through and through, full of lust and deception. Instead, there must be a spiritual renewal of your thoughts and attitudes. You must display a new nature because you are a new person, created in God's likeness—righteous, holy, and true."

10. Esther 1:4–7 NIV, emphasis mine.

11. See Psalm 100:4.

12. Although it is not my intention to develop a detailed teaching on the specific

theological or academic differences between biblical praise and biblical worship, I will briefly explain the foundations of my comments about them in this book. We begin with these passages from the *New King James Version:* Psalm 138:1–2: "I will praise You with my whole heart; before the gods I will sing praises to You. I will worship toward Your holy temple." Psalm 100:4: "Enter into His gates with thanksgiving, and into His courts with praise." *Praise (yadah* in the Hebrew) involves the extending of the hands in reverence and worship with confession of God's "worth-ship." *Singing praises (zamar* in the Hebrew) refers to the playing of instruments accompanied by the voice in celebration and song. *Worship (shachah* in the Hebrew) refers to the prostration of the body in a crouch or deep bow in respect, submission, and surrender in homage to God or royalty.

13. Revelation 4:8–11 NLT, emphasis mine.

14. James Strong, *Strong's Exhaustive Concordance of the Bible* (Peabody, Mass: Hendrickson Publishers, n.d.), Greek #4352, from #4314 and #2965; *proskuneo* or "worship."

15. Mark 10:15.

16. See Revelation 3:21.

17. The incense burners are clearly apparent in an existing bas-relief of Darius I giving an audience, found at the royal city of Persepolis. Also visible are the crown prince, Xerxes, standing immediately behind the throne, and a guard with an axe, standing behind him. A contemporary reproduction of this bas-relief and explanatory text also appear in "The Persian Empire," *Children's Encyclopedia of History: First Civilisations to the Fall of Rome* (London: Usborne Publishing, Ltd., 1985), 66.

18. Ibid. See also Jobes, who notes, "Archaeological evidence shows that [Esther's] trepidation was not unwarranted. Two bas-reliefs have been excavated from Persepolis showing a Persian king seated on his throne with a long scepter in his right hand. An attendant standing behind the throne is a Median soldier holding a large ax." The author cites as the source, Edwin M. Yamauchi, *Persia and the Bible* (Grand Rapids, Mich.: Baker Book House, 1990), 360.

19. Mark 5:24b–25, emphasis mine.

20. Mark 5:27, 29, emphasis mine.

21. Jobes, 78, citing Loeb Classical Library: Herodotus, 1.99; 3.77, 84.

22. Cook, 146.

23. Romans 3:23 KJV, emphasis mine.

24. Leviticus 16:12–13 NLT, emphasis mine.

25. See John 21:20–24.

26. Luke 7:44–47 NIV, emphasis mine.

27. See Matthew 26:6–13; Mark 14:3–9; John 12:1–8.

28. See John 20.

29. Psalm 25:14a NIV.

30. Luke 7:37–39, emphasis mine.

31. See John 4:4–42.

Chapter 4

1. Paul told Timothy, "Therefore I exhort first of all that supplications, prayers, intercessions, and giving of thanks be made for all men, for kings and all who are in authority, that we may lead a quiet and peaceable life in all godliness and reverence" (1 Timothy 2:1–2). Notice that even in this classic declaration, the "giving of thanks" shows up as a "saturating factor" that should be done throughout the prayer process. Some times appear to be better than others where prayer is concerned: "For this shall

every one that is godly pray unto thee *in a time when thou mayest be found*" (Psalm 32:6 KJV, emphasis mine).

2. See the words of Jesus in John 3:16.

3. 1 Corinthians 12:31, emphasis mine.

4. See Matthew 6:8. In this passage Jesus has just compared the mindless mass repetition employed in the prayers of those who do not know God with the prayers of a child of God. Then Jesus instructs the disciples in how to pray what is commonly called "The Lord's Prayer" as a model for intimate prayer to the Father by His sons and daughters: "Our Father . . ."

5. God reveals the truth about *prayer by relationship* in this unforgettable passage from the book of Romans: "So you should not be like cowering, fearful slaves. You should behave instead like God's very own children, adopted into his family—calling him 'Father, dear Father.' For his Holy Spirit speaks to us deep in our hearts and tells us that we are God's children" (Romans 8:15–16 NLT).

6. Esther 2:21–23 NLT, emphasis mine.

7. See Numbers 14:11–20.

8. See 2 Corinthians 3:7.

9. See Exodus 33:18–20.

10. See Matthew 17:1–3.

11. See Matthew 14:23; 26:36; John 5:19–23, 30, 36; 8:16, 28–29, 38; 10:32; 14:31; 15:15. (And this is only a partial list!)

12. Tommy Tenney, *God's Eye View* (Nashville: Thomas Nelson, 2002), 75.

13. Ibid., 76.

14. The Jewish historian Josephus records a letter written by King Xerxes to Esdras, the priest, permitting Jews throughout the Persian kingdom to return to Jerusalem if they so chose. In the copy of the letter included in Josephus, Xerxes also allotted funds from his treasury to "make as many vessels of silver and gold as thou pleasest" for the temple (Josephus, *Antiquities of the Jews*, Book XI, chapter 5, para. 1b). The next paragraph indicates that this took place in the seventh year of Xerxes' reign and that the king's gifts and the money he allowed them to confiscate from their former Babylonian captors amounted to 650 talents of silver, vessels of gold equal to 20 talents, and vessels of a highly valued alloy of gold, brass, or copper called *aurichalcum,* equal in weight to 12 talents (ibid., para. 2b.). *Author's Note:* Josephus placed the writing of this pro-Jewish letter in the *seventh year* of Xerxes' reign, the same year, according to the Bible, that the king chose and married Esther. This took place *before* the rise of Haman to prime minister in the *twelfth year* of Xerxes' reign (Esther 2–3), the year that Xerxes granted Haman's request and issued an obviously anti-Semitic death decree against the Jews.

Chapter 5

1. Understand that I'm taking poetic license when I call Esther a "peasant girl." It is likely that Mordecai was quite wealthy, and historical sources (such as Josephus) imply that he was a leading figure in the Jewish community at Babylon and later in Susa. This means that, in reality, Esther was probably well dressed and versed in all of the niceties of proper attire and demeanor. Yet she was *still* unprepared for life in the palace of King Xerxes. My point is that no matter how sophisticated, well dressed, or wealthy we may be in this life, we are in no way prepared to enter the presence of our holy God without supernatural help from the Holy Spirit.

2. See Esther 2:8.

3. Simultaneously with this writing, I am writing, in novel form, an exciting fictionalized account of the life of Esther titled *Hadassah: A Night With the King,* to be published by Bethany House Publishers, a division of Baker Books.

4. This may have helped initially conceal Hadassah's Jewish roots. Whatever the case, history would forever know her as Esther. ("Hadassah" is derived from the Hebrew root word for "myrtle," and "Esther" was rendered "Ester" in Persian, perhaps from *Ishtar,* a Mesopotamian goddess of fertility and war.) Amazingly enough, some of the Hebrew captives in Babylon—including Daniel and company—made special requests regarding food but were compliant with name changes.

5. Esther 2:7.

6. My conclusion was drawn from definitions of the original Hebrew words from *Strong's:* "*fair* or beautiful, Hebrew #3303, *yapheh,* yaw-FEH; from Hebrew #3302; beautiful (lit. or fig.): + beautiful, beauty, comely, fair (-est, one), + goodly, pleasant, well; [and] *beautiful,* Hebrew #896, *towb,* tobe; from Hebrew #2895; good (as an adj.) in the widest sense; used likewise as a noun, both in the masc. and the fem., the sing. and the plur. (good, a good or good thing, a good man or woman; the good, goods or good things, good men or women), also as an adv. (well): beautiful, best, better, bountiful, cheerful, at ease, X fair (word), (be in) favour, fine, glad, good (deed, -lier, liest, -ly, -ness, -s), graciously, joyful, kindly, kindness, liketh (best), loving, merry, X most, pleasant, + pleaseth, pleasure, precious, prosperity, ready, sweet, wealth, welfare, (be) well ([-favoured])."

7. C. F. Keil, of the Keil and Delitzsch commentaries, helps us understand that these words [from Esther 2:12 about oil, myrrh, spices, and cosmetics] mean "to rub, to polish, signifies purification and adornment with all kind of precious ointments." From Swindoll, *Esther: A Woman of Strength and Dignity,* 35, citing C. F. Kiel, *Commentary on the Old Testament in Ten Volumes, Vol. III* (Grand Rapids, Mich.: William B. Eerdmans, 1966), 334.

8. Ezra 6:9–10 KJV, emphasis mine.

9. "We 'pedestalize' people whom God has anointed. Whom does God memorialize? Jesus says that what Mary did will 'be told for a memorial of her' (Matthew 26:13). We like the anointed; He likes the 'anointers'! These are people of His face and feet—oil pourers, tear washers, humble lovers of Him more than lovers of things." (From Tommy Tenney, *The God Chasers* (Shippensburg, Penn.: Destiny Image, 1998), 133.

10. *The God Chasers,* 43.

11. See John 4:23–24.

12. Psalm 42:1–2.

13. *The God Chasers,* 42.

14. Let me clarify this point for the reader: It should be assumed and understood that the blood of Jesus Christ and His finished work on the cross is the chief qualifier and crucifier of human flesh. If these are rejected, then no amount of praise or worship by unrepentant and unredeemed flesh will make men or women fit for the presence of God. *However,* even redeemed, blood-bought believers often offer unacceptable gifts to God. Praise and worship possess the power to lift us beyond our *self*—our self-centeredness and our selfishness—to a higher realm of God-centeredness and Christlikeness. The Old Testament types and shadows offer us powerful insights into the role of praise and worship in the purification of the church and the ongoing perfection of the saints.

15. Esther 2:1 NLT, emphasis mine.

Chapter 6

1. See Acts 10:34–35 KJV.
2. Esther 2:15 KJV, emphasis mine.
3. *Strong's,* "*chamberlain,*" Hebrew #5631, *cariyc* or *caric;* from an unused root meaning "to castrate; a eunuch; by implication valet (especially of the female apartments), and thus a minister of state: chamberlain, eunuch, officer." (Acts 12:20 highlights the great importance of the *chamberlain* of Herod Agrippa in the New Testament era. People from Tyre and Sidon asked *the king's chamberlain,* Blastus, to mediate with Herod on their behalf.)
4. Ibid., "*keeper,*" Hebrew #8104. *shamar.*
5. Esther 2:8–9 NLT, emphasis mine.
6. Esther 2:9 KJV.
7. Swindoll, *Esther: A Woman of Strength and Dignity,* 45, emphasis mine.
8. Esther 2:20, emphasis mine.
9. Jobes, 96, citing Megillah 15a.
10. Esther 2:12–13, 15 NLT, emphasis mine.
11. James 1:22.
12. According to *Merriam-Webster's Collegiate Dictionary* (699), the usage of the *common term* "Star of David," or *Magen Dawid* (the shield of David) first appeared in 1904. A detailed article in *The Jewish Encyclopedia,* entitled "Magen Dawid," by Joseph Jacobs and Ludwig Blau, notes the discovery of a Star of David (or *magen dawid,* "shield of David") as early as the third century on a tombstone found in Tarentum, Italy. [See *http://jewishencyclopedia.com/view_page.jsp?artid=38&letter=M &search=magen_dawid.* Accessed 10 July 2002.] I've alluded to modern terminology for this symbol to help us understand and highlight the way God caused Esther, the Jewish maiden, to stand out from all of the rest of the bridal candidates in the Persian court—not because she *did* more but because she *was* more. She was a chosen vessel of God, and His anointing upon her set her apart and captivated the heart of Xerxes.
13. Geoffrey Wigoder, gen. ed., *Illustrated Dictionary & Concordance of the Bible* (Jerusalem: The Reader's Digest Association, Inc., with the permission of The Jerusalem Publishing House Ltd., 1986), 322–23.
14. See Matthew 14:17–21; 15:34–39.
15. Ephesians 4:11–13 NASB, emphasis mine.
16. Isaiah 64:6–7a NKJV, emphasis mine.
17. See Matthew 6:8.

Chapter 7

1. Isaiah 61:3.
2. Luke 1:28.
3. Galatians 4:19 NLT, emphasis mine.
4. Esther 4:14.
5. Esther 2:19–23 NLT, emphasis and insert mine.
6. King Xerxes led a massive army and navy campaign against Greece in 480 B.C. His navy won a decisive victory off Artemisium, and his army defeated the Spartan force trying to hold the pass at Thermopylae. Then he entered Athens and destroyed Athenian temples. Things went badly, though, at the Bay of Salamis, where King Xerxes watched from an overlooking position as one-third to one-half of his navy was destroyed (September 29, 480 B.C.). Without the navy, he could no longer support such a large army, so he took part of the army to conquer more territories in Asia

Minor (including Thessalonica) and quelled rebellions in Babylon and in Egypt. *This may account for the time that passed from Mordecai's lifesaving good deed and the sudden rise of Haman.* It is possible that Haman's actions during this long span of fighting helped elevate him to the top of Persian society. It may also explain why Esther doesn't seem to be sure of her favor with the king, who may have been dealing with the stinging feelings of defeat in the wars at the time. (Extrapolated from information in the Bible and from historical notes found in the article "Herodotus' Histories, the Twenty-Fourth Logos: Salamis," accessed via the Internet at *www.livius.org/he-hg/herodotus/logos8_24.html* on 18 October 2002.)

7. According to Herodotus, book III (30, 61–88), and Darius's own Behistun inscription, Darius participated in the "conspiracy of the Seven Persians" and helped overthrow the seven-month rule of the "Magi" (or pagan priests) who seized control of the empire after the death of King Cambyses II. Darius managed to become king, and another Persian prince moved in to round out the circle of seven "princes of the face" who were close to the king and wielded great power. They were allowed to approach the king unbidden anywhere but in his bedchambers when he was with a woman. As we noted briefly (in chapter 3), a *new official position* emerged under Darius, the holder of which had *even greater power and authority* with the king than did the seven princes. This "prime minister" or "master of the audiences" usually won his position through great military exploits or through some extraordinary personal service to the king. This appears to explain how non-Persians such as Haman and Mordecai managed to leap past the power and prestige of the seven princes of the face to become second in the Persian kingdom, after the king. (Extrapolated from information found in J. M. Cook, *The Persian Empire* (London: Schocken Books, by agreement with J. M. Dent & Sons, Ltd., 1983), 18, 143–44.)

8. Esther 3:1–2 NLT, emphasis mine.
9. Luke 2:52.
10. Deuteronomy 8:18 NLT, emphasis mine.
11. Luke 9:23–24 NLT, emphasis mine.
12. Swindoll, 148–49, emphasis mine.
13. Esther 4:13–14 NLT, emphasis mine.
14. Esther 4:15–16 NLT, emphasis mine.

Chapter 8

1. See Esther 4:1–3.
2. Esther 3:1–2 NLT, emphasis and insert mine.
3. 1 John 4:4 KJV.
4. It is, nevertheless, virtually certain that Mordecai had to bow before King Xerxes whenever he passed by Mordecai's place of service at the king's gate—or else die instantly. History records that other Jewish leaders bowed before foreign rulers simply out of protocol (Jobes, 119), much as Americans bow to the queen of England out of courtesy and respect.
5. The most telling appearance of the name "Agag" can be traced all the way back in the Scriptures to Saul and Moses (and perhaps to Esau). According to Adele Berlin, commentator for *The JPS Bible Commentary: Esther* ([Philadelphia: The Jewish Publication Society, 2001], 34): "The Amalekite connection [of Haman with the Amalekite King *Agag*] is reinforced in the synagogue lectionary cycle according to which, on the Sabbath preceding Purim, the passage in Deuteronomy 25:17–19 ('Remember what Amalek did to you. . . . You shall blot out the memory of Amalek') and the

haftarah from 1 Samuel 15 (containing the story of Saul and Agag) are read." The commentator adds, "Both Targums reflect the Masoretic Text's Agagite origin for Haman, and go even further by extending Haman's genealogy back to Esau, echoing Genesis 36:12. They thereby extend the rivalry between Mordecai and Haman even farther back in history to Esau and Jacob."

6. 1 Samuel 15:9, 13–14, 22 NLT, emphasis mine.

7. 1 Samuel 15:32–33 NLT, emphasis and insert mine.

8. Since we are dealing with an evil spirit—the spirit of Haman—that operates through human beings rather than merely a human family line, it doesn't really matter whether Agag fathered a child who survived to Esther's day. Whether Haman was descended from some other Amalekites who survived, or whether the spirit of Agag was simply operating through Haman without any literal physical link—the results were just as deadly, and the characteristic of uncontrolled anti-Semitism was just as dominant.

9. See 1 Samuel 30 and 2 Samuel 1.

10. King Saul had been wounded by Philistine archers, but there is good evidence that he also attempted but failed to kill himself with his own sword. It was the Amalekite soldier who finished the job and shared the details with David, who then had him executed for raising his hand against Saul, the Lord's anointed. The account in 1 Samuel 31:4–5 says only that the armor bearer "realized" or believed Saul was dead; it does not say Saul *died* when he fell on his sword. First Chronicles 10:1–5 specifically says the armor bearer died but does *not* say this about Saul after he fell on his own sword. This explains what *appears* to be an inconsistency between the firsthand report of the Amalekite in 2 Samuel 1 and the thirdhand accounts of 1 Samuel and 1 Chronicles.

11. 2 Samuel 1:9 KJV.

12. Esther 3:2 NLT, emphasis mine.

13. Esther 3:7–8 NLT, emphasis mine.

14. Proverbs 16:33 NLT, emphasis mine.

15. Job 1:21 KJV.

16. Jobes, 122.

17. 1 Corinthians 2:7–8 NLT, emphasis and insert mine.

18. See Esther 3:15.

19. Jobes, 42.

20. Esther 4:11 NLT.

21. Esther 4:13–14 NLT, emphasis mine.

22. Esther's position was made even more hazardous by the tradition of Persia's powerful kings making crucial (and unchangeable) decisions while helplessly intoxicated! Karen Jobes notes, "Within our modern culture we think of drinking as a social custom, often with negative connotations. However, the Greek historian Herodotus explains the interesting fact that the Persians drank as they deliberated matters of state (cf. Esther 3:15): 'Moreover it is their [the Persians'] custom to deliberate about the gravest matters when they are drunk; and what they approve in their counsels is proposed to them the next day by the master of the house where they deliberate, when they are now sober, and if being sober they still approve it, they act thereon, but if not, they cast it aside. And when they have taken counsel about a matter when sober, they decide upon it when they are drunk' [*Herodotus* 1.133]. This custom may seem bizarre to us, but *the ancients believed intoxication put them in closer touch with the spiritual world*" (Jobes, 67–68, emphasis mine).

23. Ibid., 69, citing *Herodotus,* 7.35.
24. Jona Lendering, "Summary of and Commentary on Herodotus' Histories," book 8, from the article titled "Herodotus' Histories, the Twenty-Fourth Logos: Salamis," ccessed via the Internet at *www.livius.org/he-hg/herodotus/logos8_24.html* on 18 October 2002. See also note 6, chapter 7, of endnotes.
25. Esther 4:15–16 NIV, emphasis mine.
26. See 1 Samuel 17:38–40.
27. Esther 5:1–2 NLT, emphasis mine.
28. *The God Catchers,* 188–89.
29. Hebrews 4:16 NLT.

Chapter 9

1. Esther 5:2–3 NLT.
2. The *New American Standard Version* says Queen Esther "obtained favor in his sight," and the *New International Version of the Bible* says King Xerxes "was pleased" with Esther.
3. Esther 5:4–5 NLT, emphasis mine.
4. 2 Corinthians 10:4.
5. Esther 5:4 NLT, emphasis mine.
6. There is a detailed description of the royal garden in Esther 1:5–7 (NLT): "When it was all over, the king gave a special banquet for all the palace servants and officials—from the greatest to the least. It lasted for seven days and was held at Susa in the courtyard of the palace garden. The courtyard was decorated with beautifully woven white and blue linen hangings, fastened by purple ribbons to silver rings embedded in marble pillars. Gold and silver couches stood on a mosaic pavement of porphyry, marble, mother-of-pearl, and other costly stones. Drinks were served in gold goblets of many designs, and there was an abundance of royal wine, just as the king had commanded."
7. The splendor of Saddam Hussein's palaces revealed during the Iraqi war near this geographical region pale in comparison to how the ancient kings of Persia lived.
8. See Matthew 6:28–30.
9. "I know we often speak of getting a bird's-eye view, but wouldn't you prefer to get a God's-eye view of the things that concern you? If you get caught up in worship, your perspective changes!" (Tommy Tenney, *God's Eye View: Worshiping Your Way to a Higher Perspective* [Nashville: Thomas Nelson, 2002], 112.)
10. 1 John 4:4 KJV.
11. Esther 5:5–6 NLT, emphasis mine.
12. Psalm 23:5 NIV, emphasis mine.

Chapter 10

1. Esther 6:1 KJV, emphasis mine.
2. Matthew 7:7 KJV.
3. See 1 John 5:14–15.
4. Esther 6:1 KJV.
5. Luke 13:34b NLT.
6. Psalm 121:4 NLT.
7. Jesus said in Matthew 18:12–14 NLT: "If a shepherd has one hundred sheep, and one wanders away and is lost, what will he do? Won't he leave the ninety-nine others and go out into the hills to search for the lost one? And if he finds it, he will surely rejoice over it more than over the ninety-nine that didn't wander away! In the same

way, it is not my heavenly Father's will that even one of these little ones should perish."

8. See Genesis 2:2.
9. See Psalm 121:4.
10. See John 4:18.
11. See John 4:15.
12. See John 4:16.
13. See John 4:17.
14. John 4:23 KJV.
15. My running paraphrase of John 4:25–26.
16. John 4:32 KJV.
17. See John 4:39.
18. Esther 5:9–13 NLT, emphasis mine.
19. Esther 5:14 NLT, emphasis mine.
20. Esther 6:1–3 NLT, emphasis mine.
21. Esther 6:2–3 NLT.
22. Hebrews 6:10 NLT.
23. Esther 6:4–9 NLT, emphasis mine.
24. Esther 6:10 NLT, emphasis mine.

Chapter 11

1. Esther 5:6–8 NLT, emphasis mine.
2. Luke 15:31 NLT, emphasis mine.
3. Matthew 6:8 NLT.
4. 1 Corinthians 2:9b.
5. Esther 6:10–12 NLT, emphasis mine.
6. Esther 6:13–14 NLT, emphasis mine.
7. Isaiah 54:17.

Chapter 12

1. Finis Jennings Dake, *Dake's Annotated Reference Bible* (Lawrenceville, Ga.: Dake Publishing, 1991). Rev. Dake said of the name of God in reference to Esther 1:20: "It has been observed by many that the name of God is not found in the book of Esther. . . . However, in the ancient Hebrew text there were 5 places where the name of God was hidden, being abbreviated JHVH for JeHoVaH, 4 times, and EHYEH (I Am that I Am) once. These letters were used as acrostics in certain statements, and in 3 of the MSS, they were written larger than the rest of the text so that they stood out boldly on the scroll." Dake noted that the acrostics appear in Esther 1:20 (*All the wives shall give* . . .); 5:4 (*Let the king and Haman come this day* . . .); 5:13 (*This availeth me nothing* . . .); 7:7 (*That there was evil determined against him* . . .); and 7:5 (*Who is he, and where is he* . . .). *Note:* An *acrostic* is a written piece in which the initial or final letters of words taken in order form a word or phrase.
2. Proverbs 16:33 NLT says, "We may throw the dice, but the LORD determines how they fall."
3. Proverbs 16:18.
4. Jeremiah 29:11.
5. Esther 6:11 NLT, emphasis mine.
6. Berlin, *The JPS Bible Commentary: Esther,* 62.
7. Ibid., 63. The commentator adds this full note on Esther 6:12, where Haman hurries home with his head covered in mourning: "The word *mourning* is somewhat strange,

and the rabbis, who lost no opportunity to besmirch and humiliate Haman, told a wonderfully gross midrashic tale to explain it (see, for example, B. Megillah 16a). While Haman was leading Mordecai through the streets, Haman's daughter was standing on the roof of her house and saw the two men, one leading the other on a horse. Thinking that the man on the horse was her father, being led by Mordecai, she took a chamber pot and hurled it upon the head of the man leading the horse. He looked up and then she saw that it was her father, whereupon she fell from the roof and died."

8. Esther 6:12–13 NLT, emphasis mine.
9. Esther 7:1–6 NLT, emphasis and paragraph breaks for dialogue mine.
10. See John 10:10 NLT.
11. Hebrews 10:27.
12. Esther 7:7–8 NLT.
13. Esther 7:9 NLT.
14. Esther 7:10–8:2 NLT.
15. See Colossians 2:14–15.
16. Revelation 20:10 (NLT) says: "Then the Devil, who betrayed them, was thrown into the lake of fire that burns with sulfur, joining the beast and the false prophet. There they will be tormented day and night forever and ever." (This is what I would call "sure and certain judgment.")
17. Swindoll, 140: "There is evidence in extra-biblical literature, and I'm thinking particularly of the Greek historian Herodotus, that the property of condemned criminals reverted back to the crown. So in this case, the estate of Haman, a condemned criminal, would normally become the property of the king. But of all things, the king doesn't keep it. Instead, he gives it to Esther, who in turn gives it to Mordecai, for she now tells the king about Mordecai's relationship to her." [See Esther 8:2–3.]
18. Ephesians 4:8b.
19. Proverbs 13:22.
20. See Revelation 19:11–14.
21. Esther 8:3–6 NLT.
22. See Esther 8:7–8.
23. Matthew 16:19.
24. Esther 9:1–2 NLT, emphasis mine.
25. Esther 9:3, 5 NLT, emphasis mine.
26. Esther 9:12–13 NLT, emphasis mine.
27. Joel 2:25 NLT.
28. Philippians 2:9–11 NLT says, "Because of this, God raised him up to the heights of heaven and gave him a name that is above every other name, so that at the name of Jesus every knee will bow, in heaven and on earth and under the earth, and every tongue will confess that Jesus Christ is Lord, to the glory of God the Father."
29. See Psalm 45:7; 97:10; Amos 5:15; and Hebrews 1:9.
30. Genesis 3:15 NIV.
31. Esther 9:14–16 NLT, emphasis mine.
32. See Joshua 10:12–14.
33. Ephesians 4:26.
34. 2 Corinthians 10:4–6, emphasis mine.
35. Esther 9:22 NLT.
36. Psalm 23:5 NLT, emphasis mine.

Join the Chase

There are millions of GodChasers around the world today helping ignite fire in the hearts of people who are hungry for the presence of God. Join the Chase by getting connected with *GodChasers.network*.

Once you contact us, we will send you our monthly newsletter FREE! This will help you stay informed about upcoming GodChaser Gatherings around the world, new resources by Tommy & Jeannie Tenney to share with you and the impact GodChasers around the world are making in our world today.

Sign up by calling or writing to:

(USA Office)	(European Office)
Tommy Tenney	Tommy Tenney
GodChasers.network	GodChasers.network
Post Office Box 3355	Grace International Centre
Pineville, Louisiana 71361-3355	Leamore Lane, Walsall, WS2 7PS
Telephone: 318-442-4273	Telephone: 0870 7455796

or sign up online at www.GodChasers.net

Visit us on the Web @ www.godchasers.net for more information such as:

- Upcoming events in your area
- Monthly e-letters with special offers on GodChasers products
- "Daily dose" of Scripture portions that will enable you to read through the Bible in a year by email
- How to become a prayer partner
- New books and other product releases by Tommy Tenney
- Online daily devotions by Tommy Tenney
- And much more!